Photosynthesis and Respiration

The Green World

Photosynthesis and Respiration

William G. Hopkins

CHELSEA HOUSE
PUBLISHERS

An imprint of Infobase Publishing

Photosynthesis and Respiration

Copyright © 2006 by Infobase Publishing

Chelsea House
An imprint of Infobase Publishing
132 West 31st Street
New York NY 10001

Library of Congress Cataloging-in-Publication Data

Hopkins, William G.
   Photosynthesis and respiration/William Hopkins.
     p. cm. — (The Green World)
   ISBN: 0-7910-8561-9
 1. Photosynthesis—Juvenile literature. 2. Plants—Photorespiration—Juvenile literature. I. Title. II. Series.
   QK882.H68 2006
   572'.46—dc22   2005019383

Chelsea House books are available at special discounts when purchased in bulk quantities for businesses, associations, institutions, or sales promotions. Please call our Special Sales Department in New York at (212) 967-8800 or (800) 322-8755.

You can find Chelsea House on the World Wide Web at http://www.chelseahouse.com

Text and cover design by Keith Trego

Printed in the United States of America

Bang 21C 10 9 8 7 6 5 4 3 2 1

This book is printed on acid-free paper.

All links, web addresses, and Internet search terms were checked and verified to be correct at the time of publication. Because of the dynamic nature of the web, some addresses and links may have changed since publication and may no longer be valid.

Table of Contents

Introduction

By William G. Hopkins

"Have you thanked a green plant today?" reads a popular bumper sticker. Indeed we should thank green plants for providing the food we eat, fiber for the clothing we wear, wood for building our houses, and the oxygen we breathe. Without plants, humans and other animals simply could not exist. Psychologists tell us that plants also provide a sense of well-being and peace of mind, which is why we preserve forested parks in our cities, surround our homes with gardens, and install plants and flowers in our homes and workplaces. Gifts of flowers are the most popular way to acknowledge weddings, funerals, and other events of passage. Gardening is one of the fastest growing hobbies in North America and the production of ornamental plants contributes billions of dollars annually to the economy.

Human history has been strongly influenced by plants. The rise of agriculture in the fertile crescent of Mesopotamia brought previously scattered hunter-gatherers together into villages. Ever since, the availability of land and water for cultivating plants has been a major factor in determining the location of human settlements. World exploration and discovery was driven by the search for herbs and spices. The cultivation of new world crops—sugar, cotton, and tobacco—was responsible for the introduction of slavery to America, the human and social consequences of which are still with us. The push westward by English colonists into the rich lands of the Ohio River valley in the mid-1700s was driven by the need to increase corn production and was a factor in precipitating the French and Indian War. The Irish Potato Famine in 1847 set in motion a wave of migration, mostly to North America, that would reduce the population of Ireland by half over the next 50 years.

As a young university instructor directing biology tutorials in a classroom that looked out over a wooded area, I would ask each group of students to look out the window and tell me what they saw. More often than not the question would be met with a blank, questioning look. Plants are so much a part of our environment and the fabric of our everyday lives that they rarely register in our conscious thought. Yet today, faced with disappearing rainforests, exploding population growth, urban sprawl, and concerns about climate change, the productive capacity of global agricultural and forestry ecosystems is put under increasing pressure. Understanding plants is even more essential as we attempt to build a sustainable environment for the future.

The Green World series opens doors to the world of plants. The series describes what plants are, what plants do, and where plants fit into the overall scheme of things. This present book explores the flow of energy through plants and shows how plants convert that energy to the food that sustains us all.

1 Harvesting the Sun

The sun, with all those plants revolving around it and dependent upon it,
can still ripen a bunch of grapes as if it had nothing else in the universe to do.

—Galileo

Harvesting the Sun

IT'S ALL ABOUT ENERGY

Biology students at almost all levels are familiar with proteins, DNA, and the basic mechanism of heredity. That is because, for the past several decades, the study of functional biology has been dominated by molecular biology, a particular viewpoint that attempts to explain life in terms of proteins, nucleic acids, and other large molecules (macromolecules). The conceptual framework for molecular biology was laid in the 1960s, following the discovery of the structure of the genetic material deoxyribonucleic acid (DNA) by James Watson and Francis Crick. But cells are much more than a jumble of macromolecules. Cells are a very highly organized system. They have the capacity to manipulate macromolecules, break down food, assemble complex structures, grow, reproduce, and react to their environment. The mysterious force that enables cells to do all these things, the force that literally breathes life into this jumble of macromolecules, is called energy.

The source of this life-giving energy is the sun (Figure 1.1). The sun emits most of its energy as light, a small fraction of which streams 94 million miles (150,000 km) through space until it is intercepted by the leaves of green plants here on Earth. In the cells of those leaves are microscopic structures called **chloroplasts**. Chloroplasts contain the green pigment **chlorophyll**, which absorbs the incoming solar energy and sets into motion that truly remarkable cascade of energy-transforming reactions we know as photosynthesis. The mechanisms used by plants to capture and transform this energy and how they use it to build organic matter are the subject of this book.

PLANTS ARE "DO-IT-YOURSELF" ORGANISMS

Photosynthesis is arguably the most important chemical process on the Earth, as far as the biosphere is concerned. Only through photosynthesis can light energy be captured and converted into the chemical energy that all other organisms need to survive.

Figure 1.1 The sun is a giant solar furnace. Virtually all living organisms depend on energy from the sun, which is harvested by green plants.

Nutritionally, plants are autotrophs (from the Greek words *auto* meaning "self" and *trophe* meaning "nourishment"): they are able to utilize energy from sunlight to assemble organic molecules from completely inorganic sources (carbon dioxide and water). That is why it is called photosynthesis, from the Greek words *photo*, meaning "light," and *synthesis*, meaning "to put together." Because plants and other photosynthetic organisms use light to drive their carbon nutrition, they are called photoautotrophs. Animals, on the other hand, are heterotrophs—they obtain the energy that they need only by feeding on energy-rich organic molecules that originated in plants.

In addition to energy, photosynthesis is also the sole source of the organic carbon that all carbon-based life forms, including ourselves, use to build the stuff of their existence. The term *organic* refers to compounds of carbon, excluding carbon dioxide. It is derived from the fact that organic compounds, in general, are those typically formed by living organisms. It has been estimated that every year, global conversion of inorganic carbon to organic carbon by aquatic and land-based photosynthetic organisms totals approximately 10^{11} metric tons or 100 billion metric tons (1 metric ton = 1,000 kilograms or 2,204 pounds).

Photosynthesis, however, is only half the story. Photosynthesis is limited to harvesting sunlight and storing the energy in the chemical bonds of sugars. No organism, not even a green plant, is able to use light energy directly for the synthesis of macromolecules and all of the other work that must be done by its cells. That is where **cellular respiration** comes in. Cellular respiration is a metabolic process that retrieves the energy from sugars and other organic molecules and transforms it into a molecule that is immediately available to work in the cell. This molecule, called **adenosine triphosphate (ATP)**, is the principal currency for energy transactions in cells. We will have more to say about what ATP is and how it works in Chapter 2.

PHOTOSYNTHESIS AND RESPIRATION— TWO SIDES OF THE ENERGY COIN

Photosynthesis may be thought of as a straightforward chemical reaction in which carbon dioxide from the air and water from the soil combine to produce carbohydrate (expressed as $[CH_2O]$) and oxygen according to the general equation:

$$CO_2 + H_2O + energy\ (light) \longrightarrow [CH_2O] + O_2$$

The solar energy is stored in the chemical bonds of the carbohydrate molecule, usually a simple sugar such as glucose.

Sugars, by the way, are a particularly convenient way to package both energy and carbon. Sugars may be used immediately in the leaf cells or, alternatively, they may be stored as starch in the chloroplast until their energy and carbon are needed later. Otherwise, because they are small, chemically stable molecules, sugars are readily transported to other cells and tissues, where they may be again stored as starch or used for the immediate energy and carbon needs of cells.

Light travels at a speed of 3×10^8 m s^{-1} in a vacuum. Approximately how long does it take for light to travel the distance from the sun to the earth?

The other side of the energy coin is respiration. Respiration is a sequence of enzyme-mediated reactions that all cells, including photosynthetic leaf cells, use to retrieve the solar energy and carbon stored in sugars and starch. Respiration uses about 55 different steps in total to break down the sugars into carbon dioxide and water. The reasons for so many steps are two-fold. First, the release of energy is controlled. The complete combustion of one **mole** (180 g) of glucose, for example, releases 2823 kJ (kilojoules) (675 k calories) of energy. If that energy were released all at once, the cell would literally burn up. Breaking respiration down into many small steps ensures that the energy is released in smaller quantities that can be put to work usefully in the cell. The general equation for respiration is:

$$[CH_2O] + O_2 \longrightarrow CO_2 + H_2O + energy \text{ (ATP)}$$

Note that the equation for respiration *appears* to be essentially the reverse of photosynthesis. This is superficially true. Photosynthesis and respiration are complementary halves of a carbon dioxide/sugar cycle (Figure 1.2) and many of the principles and players used in both processes are similar, if

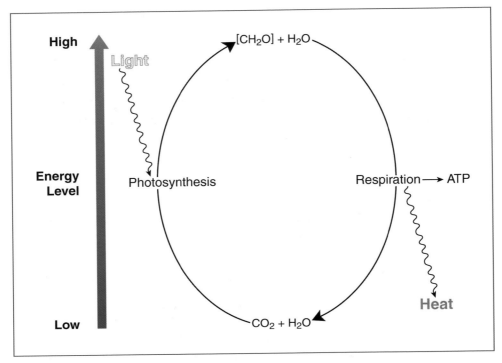

Figure 1.2 The potential energy content of sugar (CH_2O) is higher than carbon dioxide (CO_2). The difference is made up by the input of light energy through photosynthesis. Energy stored in carbohydrates is retrieved by respiration, which breaks down the sugar to carbon dioxide and water. Some of the energy is released as heat and the rest is stored in molecules such as ATP, which carry the energy to other regions of the cell to power other cellular functions.

not the same. But, as we shall see in later chapters, the overall reactions are quite different.

PHOTOSYNTHESIS GENERATES OXYGEN

The equation for photosynthesis reveals a very significant "side effect"—one of the "waste" products of photosynthesis is molecular oxygen. For this reason, photosynthesis in green plants is referred to as oxygenic. This factor is important because when the Earth was first formed, there was probably no free oxygen. Most of the oxygen was tied up as oxides of hydrogen (i.e., water), silicon (i.e., quartz sand), calcium, iron, and a host of other mineral elements. Until oxygenic photosynthesis by green plants appeared on the scene, there was no free oxygen to support the evolution of heterotrophic animal life. Indeed, virtually all of the oxygen that supports animal life—including humans—has been generated by oxygenic photosynthesis over the millennia. This idea is pursued further in Chapter 7.

THE DARK SIDE OF PHOTOSYNTHESIS

As early as 1905, evidence began to accumulate indicating that photosynthesis was a two-stage process. Early studies were conducted by the English plant physiologist F. F. Blackman, who studied the combined effects of light and temperature on the rate of photosynthesis. Blackman's experiments indicated that there was one set of reactions that was limited by the amount of available light but was insensitive to temperature. A second set of reactions did not require light but was accelerated by increasing the temperature to a maximum of 30°C (86°F). Both the light-dependent and light-independent reactions were obviously necessary and maximum photosynthesis could be achieved only with a combination of high light and high temperature.

Insensitivity to temperature is characteristic of purely physical reactions, such as the absorption of light by a pigment and related photochemical reactions. On the other hand, sensitivity to temperature is characteristic of chemical and biochemical reactions, especially those that involve the participation of the biochemical catalysts called enzymes. Later experiments using brief flashes of light demonstrated that the amount of photosynthesis per flash depended on the amount of light (i.e., the intensity of the flash) but also on the length of the dark period between flashes. Maximum efficiency in the use of the light energy in each flash was achieved with a dark interval of about 0.1 second. This was clear evidence that photosynthesis takes place in two stages. The first stage is a set of rapid, light-dependent reactions, or "**light reactions**," which convert light energy to chemical energy. The second stage is a set of slower, light-independent, enzyme-catalyzed reactions, the so-called **dark reactions**, which use the chemical energy produced during the light reactions to convert carbon dioxide to sugar (Figure 1.3).

The term *dark reactions* can be misleading as it implies that these reactions occur only in the dark, but that is not the case. The expression "dark reactions" originally meant only that there was no evidence that these reactions were light-driven. Indeed, for two reasons, the dark reactions come to a halt almost immediately after the light is extinguished. The first reason is that the dark reactions proceed only while a pool of energy-rich products from the light reactions is available. These products are produced only in the light, do not accumulate to any significant extent, and are very short-lived. The second reason is that several of the enzymes that catalyze key steps in the dark reactions, while they are not light-driven, must first be activated by light before they will work. It is one way that cells in the plant ensure that resources are not committed to metabolic processes that can not go on during extended dark periods (at night, for instance).

For these reasons, the term *dark reactions* has fallen out of favor. The preferred term is now *carbon fixation reactions*, a term based on the idea that when carbon dioxide is first incorporated into organic compounds, the carbon dioxide is said to have been "fixed."

A LEAF IS A SOLAR SUGAR FACTORY

Leaves exist for no other reason than to carry out photosynthesis. Indeed, a leaf may be viewed as a highly efficient photosynthetic factory dedicated solely to the manufacture of sugar. Like any successful factory, leaves require the appropriate machinery, a supply of energy to run the machinery, an efficient ("just-in-time

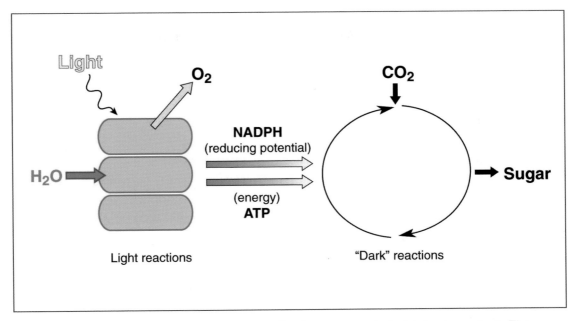

Figure 1.3 The two stages of photosynthesis are separate but interdependent. The light-dependent reactions (left), based in the chloroplast membranes, harvest solar energy and store it as chemical energy (NADPH and ATP). The stored energy is then used by enzymes of the carbon fixation reactions ("dark reactions") to synthesize sugar from carbon dioxide.

delivery") supply of raw materials, and a system for efficient distribution of the product.

Photosynthesis is driven by solar energy and leaves are a model of efficiency as solar collectors. A typical leaf, for example, is broad and thin, much like the solar panel that heats your neighbor's swimming pool or powers a space satellite. The broad surface of the leaf is almost always presented to the sun for maximum light interception. Solar tracking by sunflowers is well known, but the leaves of many plants exhibit a similar behavior. Many plants, in fact, continually reorient their leaves during the day in order to track the sun and maintain maximal light interception. In addition, leaves are generally thin in order to limit attenuation of the light reaching the lowermost cells. It would be of little value to have photosynthetic machinery at the lower surface of a leaf if the light were completely absorbed before it got there. Moreover, the optical properties of leaves ensure that the light takes an erratic path once it enters the leaf, thus increasing the probability that the light will eventually strike and be absorbed by a molecule of chlorophyll. Finally, in most plants, leaves are positioned on the stem so that lower leaves in the canopy are shaded as little as possible by the leaves above them.

The two surfaces of a leaf are covered with a layer of cells called the **epidermis** (Figure 1.4). Epidermal cells are very tightly packed with no intercellular spaces. In surface view, the epidermal cells are often irregularly shaped, resembling a layer of interlocking paving stones. Epidermal cells contain no chloroplasts and, like your own epidermis (or skin), their principal function is to provide mechanical protection.

Located between the two epidermal layers are two kinds of photosynthetic mesophyll (from *meso*, meaning middle, and *phyll*, meaning leaf) cells. On the upper side of the leaf are one or possibly two layers of closely packed, columnar cells called **palisade mesophylls**. Palisade cells contain a large number of chloroplasts and are responsible for most of the photosynthesis that occurs in the leaf. Below the palisade cells are the **spongy mesophylls**, which are much more irregular in shape and are surrounded by a system of interconnected air spaces. The air spaces facilitate gas exchange, such as the uptake of carbon dioxide and the release of oxygen.

The leaf is connected to the stem by a leaf stalk, or petiole, that contains a major vein of vascular tissue. The term *vascular* refers to the conducting tissues through which water, minerals, and small organic molecules move between plant organs such as roots and leaves. This large vein is continuous with the vascular system of the stem and roots to facilitate the distribution of water and solutes throughout the plant. In the leaf blade, the vein

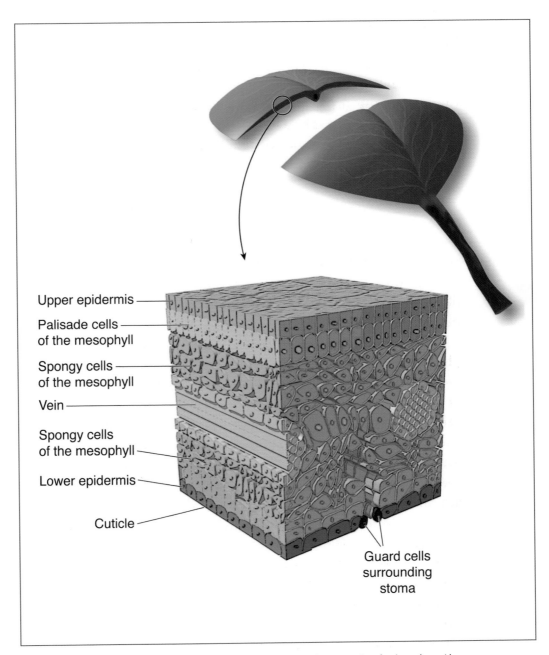

Upper epidermis

Palisade cells
of the mesophyll

Spongy cells
of the mesophyll

Vein

Spongy cells
of the mesophyll

Lower epidermis

Cuticle

Guard cells
surrounding
stoma

Figure 1.4 A cross section of a dicotyledonous leaf showing the epidermis and both the palisade and spongy mesophyll cells.

subdivides extensively, so that almost every photosynthetic cell has direct contact with a small vein. The close proximity of photosynthetic cells to the veins is important because half of the vascular tissue, the xylem, supplies the cells with the water and minerals necessary to support photosynthesis and other cellular activities. The other half of the vascular tissue, the phloem, carries the products of photosynthesis to the stems, roots, flowers, and other organs.

> **Can you see where the xylem and phloem fit into our analogy of the leaf as a photosynthetic factory?**

THE COMPLEXITY OF CHLOROPLASTS

The site of photosynthesis in the cell is a discrete structure, or organelle (little organ), called the chloroplast. Chloroplasts are the machinery referred to in the factory analogy. As cellular organelles go, chloroplasts are about medium-sized: they are much smaller than nuclei or vacuoles, and quite a bit larger than ribosomes. Chloroplasts in the leaves of higher plants are shaped like a disk or wafer with a diameter of about 5.0 micrometers (μm) (Figure 1.5). At this size, about 200 chloroplasts could be lined up across the head of a straight pin. Although very small in size, their large numbers means that, in aggregate, chloroplasts can be very productive. A typical leaf cell will contain 20 to 60 chloroplasts and a section of a corn leaf 1 millimeter square may contain as many as half a million. It has been estimated that all of the chloroplasts in a typical mature sugar maple tree could have a total surface area of more than 360 square kilometers (140 square miles) and produce as much as two tons of sugar per day!

A chloroplast is bound by a pair of outer membranes, called the envelope (Figure 1.6). The two envelope membranes contain transport proteins that control the molecular traffic between the chloroplast and its surroundings. The most striking feature of chloroplasts, however, is an extensive network of internal

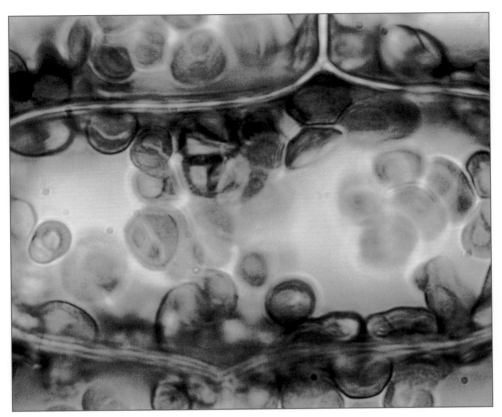

Figure 1.5 Under a light microscope, chloroplasts appear as disk-shaped green objects.

membranes. These membranes form a system of flattened sacs—like squashed balloons—called **thylakoids**, which traverse the chloroplast from one end to the other. The space inside the thylakoid is called the **lumen**. The thylakoid membranes contain the chlorophyll and are the site of the light reactions of photosynthesis, although, as we will see in Chapter 3, the lumen also plays a critical role.

Most chloroplasts, but not all, are characterized by regions where the thylakoids overlap and form, in cross section, disk-like stacks that have been likened to a stack of coins. These stacks are called grana. Unfortunately, an electron microscope only

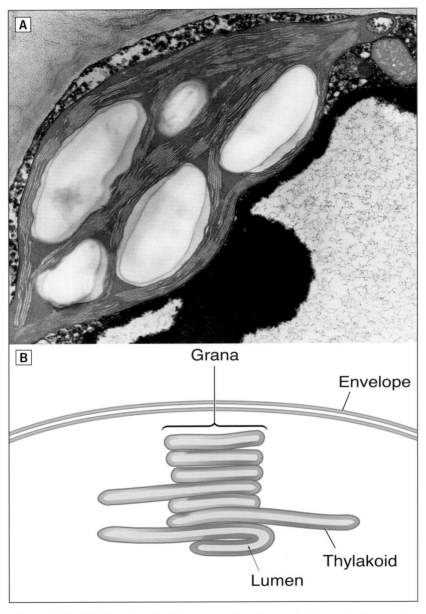

Figure 1.6 (A) The detailed internal structure of chloroplasts can be seen in the electron microscope. The opaque structures are starch grains. (B) Clearly visible are the double outer envelope and the thylakoid membranes that are stacked to form grana.

allows us to look at thylakoids in cross section. If we could view thylakoids in three dimensions, we would probably see that all of the thylakoid membranes are part of a single, continuous, and overlapping membrane system.

The homogeneous region in which the thylakoids are embedded is called the **stroma**. The principal constituents of the stroma are proteins, most of which are enzymes of the carbon fixation cycle. The stroma also contains complete genetic machinery, including nucleic acids and the ribosomes on which proteins are formed. Although not part of the photosynthetic system per se, the chloroplast genome allows the chloroplast to encode and synthesize many of its own proteins. Even so, the chloroplast is not completely autonomous in a genetic sense. Most chloroplast proteins are encoded in the cell's nucleus and synthesized in the cytoplasm before being imported into the chloroplast. Curiously, many chloroplast proteins are comprised of two or more subunits, where one subunit is encoded in the chloroplast genome while the other is encoded in the nuclear genome of the host cell, then assembled into the final protein. It is believed that this situation arose because chloroplasts originated as green algae that came to live symbiotically inside early plant cells (see Chapter 7). Over time, much of the chloroplast DNA was slowly incorporated into the nuclear genome.

Chloroplasts are not present in young, actively dividing cells at the stem apex, even in those cells that will eventually give rise to leaves. Instead, all young cells contain smaller unpigmented organelles called proplastids. Proplastids are carried from one generation to the next through maternal, or egg, cells and are maintained in the undifferentiated state in the meristems, or actively growing, regions of the plant. In actively growing cells, the proplastids divide and enlarge. In flowers, fruits, and root cells, proplastids may become chromoplasts that contain deposits of carotene or other pigments. Chloroplasts may also be converted to chromoplasts in maturing tissues, as they are in

Why Are Pine Leaves Round?

In contrast to the leaves of most deciduous broadleaf species, there are many plants with leaves of different shapes that would not appear to have the same efficiency in light collection for photosynthesis. Unusual shapes are often adaptations to specific environmental situations.

For example, needle-like leaves of evergreen coniferous plants such as pines and spruces are elongated and circular in cross section. Pine needles persist for two or three years before they are shed, making them vulnerable to water loss during winter. Their shape is one of several adaptations that reduce water loss.

Water evaporates only from the surface of a body, not from its core, so another way to reduce evaporation is to minimize the surface area relative to the volume of the tissue. The rate of transpiration from the flattened leaf of a typical deciduous species may at times be quite high, in part because they present a large surface area relative to their volume. The transpiration rate for a pine needle tends to be lower because the needle-shaped leaf approximates a sphere, which is the geometric shape with the smallest ratio of surface area to volume.

The needle shape of the pine leaf also reduces the leaf's thermal load. When leaves absorb sunlight, a portion of the absorbed energy increases the temperature of the leaf. A typical deciduous leaf exposed to the summer sun may reach 5°C to 10°C above the ambient air temperature. Although they present a much smaller surface to the sun, pine needles are exposed both to direct sunlight and to light reflected from the snow. One result is that leaf temperatures as much as 20°C above that of the ambient air have been recorded on conifer leaves when the sun climbs higher in the sky in late winter or spring. Such a temperature difference could increase the driving force for transpiration.

Pine needles have several features other than shape that tend to counteract this tendency for a high transpiration rate, such as sunken stomata and a thicker cuticle. The sunken stomata and guard cells form a channel above the pore that fills with water vapor, which slows the rate of water diffusion almost ten times more than broadleaf species.

ripened tomato fruit and in orange and yellow autumn leaves. In storage tissues, proplastids may become organelles for starch deposition, called amyoplasts. In cells that are destined to become photosynthetic, however, the proplastids will accumulate **protochlorophyll**, a chlorophyll-like molecule that is converted to chlorophyll when exposed to light.

THE PHOTOSYNTHESIS-TRANSPIRATION COMPROMISE

A leaf may be a model of photosynthetic efficiency, but there are certain problems it must contend with. Principal among these is water retention. Without water, life as we know it is not possible. Water is the milieu in which the biochemistry of life is carried out and, consequently, living cells are necessarily filled with the stuff. The water content of air, however, is often quite low and, as you know from hanging your clothes out to dry, water freely evaporates from an unprotected surface. Cell walls are such a surface. The cellulose fibers that make up the wall are saturated with water, creating a potentially serious problem. The rate of water loss from an unprotected leaf would very quickly exceed the capacity of plants to re-supply water from the roots and the plant would dry out. Plants avoid this problem by coating their outer leaf surfaces with a waxy deposit called the **cuticle**. The cuticle is impervious to water, so it prevents evaporation of water from the surfaces of the epidermal cells and thus protects the plant from potentially lethal desiccation. Unfortunately, the cuticle creates a conundrum for the leaf because it is also impervious to carbon dioxide.

Leaves balance the competing needs of taking in carbon dioxide while at the same time restricting water loss through the presence of microscopic pores or **stomata** (singular, stoma) in the epidermal layers (Figure 1.7). Stomata may be found in both the upper and lower epidermis, but are usually more abundant on the lower side. Their function is to circumvent the diffusion barrier imposed by the cuticle and allow atmospheric carbon

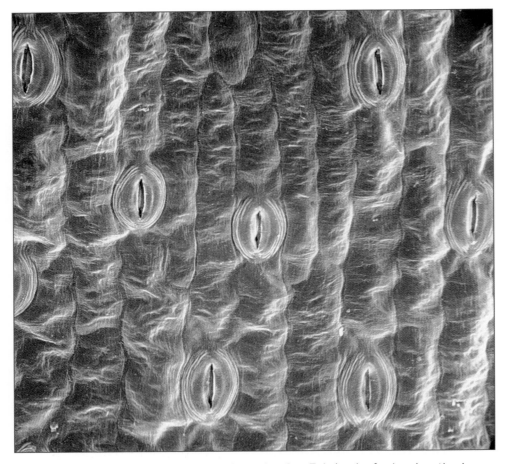

Figure 1.7 Stomata in the lower epidermis of a *Zebrina* leaf, showing the bean-shaped guard cells typical of dicotyledonous leaves.

dioxide to diffuse into the internal air spaces of the leaf. The carbon dioxide then diffuses from the air space into the mesophyll cells for use in photosynthesis.

While stomata solved the problem of getting carbon dioxide into the leaf, the problem of water loss remains. The rate of water loss from a leaf is in direct proportion to the difference in water vapor concentration, or relative humidity, between the internal atmosphere of the leaf and the ambient air. The air spaces inside the leaf are in equilibrium with the wet surfaces of the bordering mesophyll cells and so are normally saturated with water vapor. In other words, the relative humidity (RH) of the air spaces inside the leaf is always 100%. The relative humidity of the atmosphere, however, is usually less than 100% and often quite a bit less. The result is that there is almost always a large water vapor gradient between the leaf and the atmosphere. Thus, whenever the stomata are open to admit carbon dioxide into the leaf, water vapor will just as easily diffuse in the opposite direction. Even an atmospheric RH of 90% will draw considerable water vapor out of the leaf. Once again the leaf is faced with the conundrum of balancing carbon dioxide uptake and water loss.

The diffusion of water vapor out of a leaf, called **transpiration,** is controlled by a pair of guard cells that border the stoma and change their shape as a function of the water status of the leaf. Imagine two kidney beans placed with their concave sides toward each other and you have a fair image of a pair of typical guard cells in the leaf of a dicotyledonous plant (such as beans, maples, and cherry trees). Unlike the surrounding epidermal cells, guard cells are not covered by the cuticle. They also have relatively thin walls except for thickenings where the two cells abut the pore. When water is plentiful, the guard cells take up water by osmosis and become turgid, or swollen. The internal hydraulic pressure causes the thin outer walls to bulge outward, the cells bend, and the thickened walls of the two cells pull away from each other, creating a space (or pore) between them. Conversely, under conditions of water deficit, the guard cells will lose their turgor, straighten out, and the pore between them closes. The guard cells of monocotyledonous plants (such as cereals, grasses, and orchids) are shaped somewhat differently, more like a pair of barbells, but the result of increased turgor is the same: the pore opens when the thin-walled ends of the cells push against each other, thereby pushing the "handles" apart.

Guard cells respond very quickly to water stress and stomatal closure dramatically reduces water loss from the leaf before significant damage can occur. This also means that during dry weather, when the stomata are closed, the photosynthetic cells in the leaf are cut off from their supply of atmospheric carbon dioxide. Photosynthesis is then limited to recycling the carbon dioxide produced by respiration within the leaf itself. The leaf thus uses the guard cells to constantly balance water loss against carbon dioxide uptake. This transpiration-photosynthesis compromise can be an important factor limiting agricultural productivity in arid and semi-arid regions.

Under normal circumstances, stomata are open in the light and closed in the dark. The mechanism is probably related to the fact that guard cells are the only epidermal cells that contain chloroplasts. During the daylight hours, the guard cells use light energy to generate ATP, which in turn energizes potassium pumps in the cell membrane. Potassium pumps are membrane proteins that use energy to move potassium ions into the guard cells from adjacent epidermal cells. The accumulation of potassium in the guard cells is followed by the osmotic uptake of water, the guard cells swell, and the stomata open so the leaf can take in carbon dioxide. At nightfall, when carbon dioxide is no longer required, photosynthetic production of ATP in the guard cells shuts down and the pumps cease to operate. Potassium spontaneously leaks out of the guard cells, followed by the osmotic loss of water, and the stomata close. Dark closure clearly serves to limit water loss during periods when there is no need for carbon dioxide because photosynthesis is not operating.

Summary

If it can be said that plants have a purpose, it has to be photosynthesis. The architecture of a plant, and especially its leaves, appears engineered solely to facilitate the harvesting of sunlight and its storage as chemical energy in the form of sugars. Indeed, plants may be thought of as dedicated photosynthetic machines that turn photons into food for all life on Earth.

Photosynthesis occurs in two stages; a light-dependent stage and a light-independent stage. The light-dependent stage is responsible for the conversion of light energy to chemical energy and the light-independent stage uses that energy to convert carbon dioxide to sugar. Most leaves are designed to optimize the interception of light and the photosynthetic mesophyll region of the leaf is infused with small veins providing a supply of water and nutrient elements to the chloroplasts. The veins also provide a route for the export of photosynthetic products to the roots, stems, and other plant tissues.

Leaves are sheathed with epidermal cells that serve to protect the underlying mesophyll cells. The epidermal cells are coated with a waxy cuticle that is impervious to water and prevents lethal desiccation of the leaf cells. The epidermis is also perforated with small pores, or stomata, that overcome the permeability barrier of the cuticle and allow carbon dioxide from the atmosphere to diffuse into the leaf. Guard cells surrounding the pores are hydraulically operated valves that control the loss of water vapor.

2 A Short Course in Bioenergetics

Nothing can be created out of nothing.

— Lucretius (99 B.C.–5 B.C.)
Roman poet, philosopher

A Short Course in Bioenergetics

SOLAR POWER

The sun that provides the energy to drive photosynthesis is a giant thermonuclear reaction. The sun's core contains massive amounts of hydrogen at a temperature near 25 million °F. Under these conditions, protons (hydrogen nuclei stripped of their attendant electron) occasionally collide with sufficient force to initiate a fusion reaction. There are several steps to this fusion reaction, but the net result is that four protons fuse to form one helium (He) atom (Figure 2.1).

Curiously, if the mass of four hydrogen atoms (4.0316 gram-atoms) is compared with the mass of one helium atom (4.0026 gram-atoms), there is a small discrepancy. Approximately 0.029 gram-atoms of mass are missing. In fact, the missing mass has been converted to energy. Remember $E = mc^2$, Einstein's most famous equation? It tells us that mass and energy are interchangeable and, when a conversion occurs, the amount of energy released is enormous. According to Einstein's equation, the amount of energy (E) created (in watts) is equal to the mass (m, in kilograms) destroyed multiplied by the speed of light ($c = 3 \times 10^8$ meters per second) squared. The speed of light squared is 9×10^{16} or 90 million billion! A single kilogram of mass releases 90 million billion watts of power and the sun converts about 4.5 million tons of matter every second. Most of this energy is in the form of electromagnetic radiation and most of that radiation, consisting of minute packets of energy called **photons**, is in the visible portion of the spectrum, or light.

About one-third of the sunlight that reaches Earth is reflected back into space, just as sunlight is reflected from our moon. Of the remaining two-thirds, most is absorbed by soil and water on the Earth's crust and converted to heat. This heat warms the atmosphere, evaporates water to form clouds, and generally controls weather patterns worldwide. Only a very small portion of the solar radiation reaching earth, probably less than 1%, is captured by plants to be used in photosynthesis.

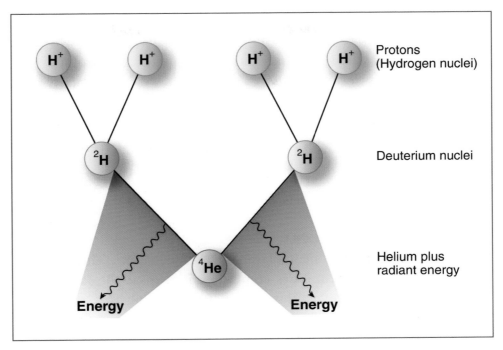

Figure 2.1 Deep in the sun's core, 300,000 miles from the surface, hydrogen atoms are fused into helium. Energy released in the form of gamma rays pours toward the surface where collisions with other gases generate ultraviolet and visible radiation.

ENERGY MUST OBEY THE LAWS OF THERMODYNAMICS

Energy is an elusive quantity—you can not see it or hold it in your hands. In fact, energy is best described not by what it is but what it does. Energy holds electrons in their orbits around atomic nuclei and holds molecules together. A flame gives off thermal energy that heats the surrounding air or burns your finger if you get too close. The energy of falling water can turn a turbine, the rotating turbine can generate electrical energy, and electrical energy creates light when you flip on your light switch. Except perhaps when stored in a battery, energy is seldom static. Energy flows and is often transformed from one form to another. Life depends on the flow of energy and energy transformations are what keep organisms alive.

Interest in the study of energy began in the 19th century through efforts to understand how steam engines worked and why heat was generated when boring out cannon barrels. These efforts gave rise to a whole new field of science called **thermodynamics,** which is used to describe the flow of energy and its various transformations. The term *thermodynamics* reflects this early interest in heat, although thermodynamic principles are broadly applicable to all forms of energy. When thermodynamic principles are invoked to help explain the flow of energy through living organisms, it is called **bioenergetics.**

THE LAW OF CONSERVATION OF ENERGY

There are two fundamental laws of thermodynamics. The first law of thermodynamics is commonly known as the law of conservation of energy. This law states quite simply that *energy cannot be created or destroyed; it can only be changed from one form to another.* Put another way, this law says that there is a constant amount of energy in the universe—whatever was there in the beginning is all there will ever be. Energy can be moved around from one place to another or changed from one form to another, but it can all be accounted for somewhere.

Water in a reservoir on the hill, gasoline in the tank of your automobile, and the food you ingest every day are all forms of stored, or potential, energy. Potential energy can be transformed to various forms of active, or kinetic, energy. When water falls from a reservoir, its potential energy is converted to kinetic energy. The kinetic energy of falling water is then converted to mechanical energy when it turns a turbine and then to electrical energy when the turbine turns a generator. The potential chemical energy of the gasoline in your automobile is converted to kinetic energy as you drive down the street. The potential energy in the food you eat is converted to kinetic energy of breathing, walking, and all the other things you do.

No energy transformations are 100% efficient. In all of the examples above, some portion of the energy is converted to heat that is dissipated into the environment. This heat energy contributes to the random motion of molecules, but is generally not available to do useful work. The first law of thermodynamics tells us that if we could add up all of the heat and all of the work that was done, the total amount of energy would equal what we started with.

THE SECOND LAW OF THERMODYNAMICS

Rolling a large boulder uphill is work. So is cleaning your room or mowing the lawn. You know intuitively that any activity that requires you to expend energy is a form of work. A physicist defines work more generally as displacement of an object against some force—rolling that boulder uphill against the force of gravity, for example, or moving an electron against the force that attracts it to an atomic nucleus. The biologist's definition of work is even broader, encompassing activities such as the synthesis of organic molecules, moving solutes across cellular membranes, osmosis, muscle contraction, and the dynamics of ecosystems. In effect, virtually any activity that consumes energy can be considered work. It should not be too surprising, then, that a biologist's principal concern with energy is whether or not that energy is available to do work.

This view simplifies things to the extent that it leaves only two kinds of energy—energy that can do work and energy that can not do work. Energy that is available to do work is called **free energy** or Gibbs free energy in honor of J. W. Gibbs, a 19th century physical chemist who introduced the concept. Free energy is assigned the symbol G. This book is about photosynthesis and respiration, so let's talk about free energy in the context of these two reactions. In the simplest possible terms, photosynthesis and respiration can be expressed as a reversible chemical reaction:

Respiration

$$C_6H_{12}O_6 + 6O_2 \longleftrightarrow 6CO_2 + 6H_2O + Energy$$

Glucose   Carbon dioxide

Photosynthesis

A molecule of glucose has a relatively high free energy, while the free energy of its equivalent in the form of six molecules of carbon dioxide and water is much lower. We don't need to know the absolute free energy values for glucose or for carbon dioxide plus water. Only the difference in free energy (expressed as ΔG) between the two states is important because that is the energy that is available to do work.

The difference in free energy between the energy of glucose and the energy of carbon dioxide plus water amounts to 2,869 kJ (686 kcal) per mole (the atomic weight of a substance, expressed in grams). When plants synthesize glucose from carbon dioxide and water, this amount of energy must be obtained from somewhere else in order to make up the difference in free energy. In photosynthesis, this energy is supplied by light. When one mole of glucose is broken down to carbon dioxide and water, the 2,869 kJ of energy is released. This is the amount of energy that is available to do work. When energy is consumed in a reaction, as it is in photosynthesis, the value of ΔG is positive. When energy is released, as it is in respiration, the value of ΔG is negative.

A reaction that proceeds with a release of free energy (ΔG negative) is called an **exergonic reaction**. A reaction that requires an input of free energy (ΔG positive) to make it happen is called an **endergonic reaction**. Put another way, an exergonic reaction is one in which the free energy of the products is less than the free energy of the reactants; an endergonic reaction is one in which the free energy of the products is greater than the free energy of the reactants.

Only exergonic reactions will occur spontaneously. Solutes will always flow from a region of higher concentration to a region of lower concentration and heat will always flow from a warm body to a cold body. The oxidation of glucose to carbon dioxide and water is a spontaneous reaction, but the reverse reaction is not. Despite the large quantities of carbon dioxide and water in the atmosphere, they have never been known to spontaneously recombine to form glucose.

Every time work is done or energy is converted from one form to another, some of the energy inevitably ends up in a form that is not available to do any further work. This form of energy is called **entropy**. Entropy is an obscure concept, usually described as a measure of disorder or randomness in a system. Whenever work is done, such as when gasoline is burned in an automobile engine, some of the energy is lost as heat that eventually dissipates into the environment. The energy of the gasoline is distinctly non-random—it is right there in the tank—but the heat generated as the gasoline is burned eventually becomes uniformly distributed throughout the universe.

As another example, consider a sugar molecule such as glucose. Glucose is highly ordered—we can predict with a fair degree of certainty the location of the six carbon atoms in the molecule at any given time. Therefore, the entropy of glucose is low. Those same six carbon atoms in the form of six individual carbon dioxide molecules, however, are free to randomize throughout the environment and their position at any point in time would be highly unpredictable. Therefore, the entropy level of the individual carbon dioxide molecules is high.

One consequence of thermodynamic laws is that spontaneous reactions always lead to an increase in entropy. This is about as much as we need to know about entropy, except perhaps to stress the inverse relationship between free energy and entropy. When the free energy level of a molecule or system is high, the entropy is low; when the free energy level is low, the entropy is high.

We can now state the second law of thermodynamics: *the entropy of the universe tends toward a maximum.* The obvious corollary is that the free energy, or the capacity for useful work, in the universe tends toward a minimum. Everything in the universe is moving inexorably toward maximum disorder or randomness.

> When you enter the shade of the forest, a significant cooling effect is often felt. What properties of leaves do you think are responsible for this effect? Would you expect the effect to be stronger in a deciduous forest or a pine forest?

If you think about it, cells (and organisms) at first seem to contravene the second law. After all, as cells grow and develop they continue to do work, build increasing order and complexity, and maintain low entropy. However, this is not really the dilemma that it first seems. The key is that cells and organisms are not isolated systems. Plants are able to increase order and maintain low entropy because of a constant input of energy from the sun. Animals eat plants or other animals that have eaten plants. Either way, living organisms continuously take in a supply of new energy from their environment in order to maximize order and minimize entropy. Only when an organism loses the capacity to take in and process energy does it become an isolated system and then maximum entropy is achieved rather quickly. Another word for maximum entropy under these circumstances is death.

OXIDATION AND REDUCTION:
USING ELECTRONS TO TRANSFER ENERGY
The key to biological energy transformations is the transfer of energy from one molecule to another. One of the two most common mechanisms for transferring energy in biochemical reactions involves the exchange of electrons between molecules. These types of reactions are known as **oxidation-reduction** (or **redox**) reactions. A loss of one or more electrons is known as **oxidation** and the molecule that loses electrons is said to be oxidized. In biochemical reactions, an oxidized molecule is

often referred to as an electron donor. Conversely, the gain of an electron is known as **reduction** and the molecule that gains the electron, the electron acceptor, is said to be reduced. Note that an oxidation-reduction reaction does not necessarily require the participation of oxygen, only that electrons be exchanged. The process is called oxidation solely because oxygen is one of the most common electron acceptors. Another point to note is that electrons can not exist in a free state, so the oxidation of one molecule must be accompanied by the reduction of another molecule.

Entropic Doom

The second law of thermodynamics can be formulated in a number of ways. The most celebrated version of the second law is the one expressed by R. J. Clausius, a 19th-century German physicist and mathematician: "The energy of the universe is constant; the entropy of the universe tends toward a maximum." Commonly known as Clausius' Dictum, the second law conveys the notion that entropy is an index of exhaustion.

As the universe ages, it steadily loses its capacity for spontaneous change (i.e., free energy decreases) and becomes progressively more disordered (i.e., entropy increases). As a result, all of the energy in the universe may one day be randomly and uniformly distributed. No stars would shine, planets would no longer rotate on their axes, and the universe would reach a state of total equilibrium, resulting in an entropic doom. However, this won't happen for a few years. The best guess tells us that the universe is 14 billion years old. The Earth formed about 5 billion years ago and the first living cells appeared about 4.5 billion years ago. The first vertebrates appeared less than 500 million years ago and humans have been around for less than one million years. It appears that our sun has at least another 5 billion years of hydrogen fuel remaining and the universe should stave off entropic doom for perhaps another 100 billion years.

> Look around. Can you see examples of oxidation in your everyday environment? (Hint: we often call the products of oxidation rust and corrosion.)

Both photosynthesis and respiration are examples of oxidation-reduction reactions. In photosynthesis, water is oxidized to molecular oxygen and the electrons are used to reduce carbon dioxide to sugar. Respiration is just the opposite—sugar or other organic molecules are oxidized and the electrons are used to reduce oxygen and form water.

An electron donor is also known as a reducing agent because, by donating electrons, it causes another molecule to become reduced. Conversely, an electron acceptor is known as an oxidizing agent. As we will see in the next chapter, one consequence of the light reactions of photosynthesis is to generate a strong reducing agent that carries sufficient energy to reduce carbon dioxide. Oxygen, on the other hand, is a strong oxidizing agent that serves as the final acceptor for electrons stripped from glucose during respiration.

In both photosynthesis and respiration, the electron transfers are not simple, one-step reactions but involve mobile electron carriers that shuttle electrons from one intermediate to another. The two most common electron carriers are **nicotinamide adenine dinucleotide** (**NAD**) and **nicotinamide adenine dinucleotide phosphate** (**NADP**) (Figure 2.2). The role of these carriers in redox reactions can be illustrated by one of the reactions in respiration. In this reaction, malic acid (or malate) is oxidized to oxaloacetic acid (or oxaloacetate). The half-reaction for malate oxidation is:

$$malate \longrightarrow oxaloacetate + 2e^- + 2H^+$$

The electrons removed from malate are transferred to NAD^+, the oxidized form of NAD, thus reducing NAD^+ to NADH. The reduction of NAD^+ is shown by the second half-reaction:

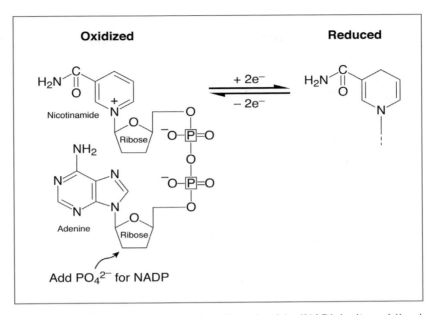

Figure 2.2 Nicotinamide adenine dinucleotide (NAD) in its oxidized form, NAD⁺, and reduced form, NADP. A molecule of NAD contains two nitrogenous bases, nicotinamide and adenine, two molecules of ribose (a 5-carbon sugar), and two phosphate groups, which form nucleotides. The nicotinamide ring exchanges electrons during oxidation-reduction reactions. The addition of two electrons reduces the number of carbon-carbon double bonds from three to two. Nicotinamide adenine dinucleotide phosphate (NADP) is similar to NAD except that an additional phosphate group is attached to the ribose in the adenine nucleotide. NAD is used in respiration while NADP is used in photosynthesis.

$$NAD^+ + 2e^- + 2H^+ \longrightarrow NADH + H^+$$

Combining these two half-reactions gives us the overall reaction in which the reduction of NAD^+ is coupled to the oxidation of malate (Figure 2.3):

$$malate + NAD^+ \longrightarrow oxaloacetate + NADH + H^+$$

NADH is a strong reducing agent that can be used to reduce another molecule elsewhere in the cell.

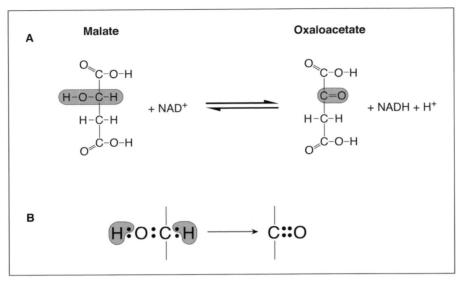

Figure 2.3 (A) The enzyme malate dehydrogenase catalyzes the transfer of electrons from malate to NAD^+. Malate is thus oxidized to oxaloacetate and NAD^+ is reduced to $NADH + H^+$. (B) A single chemical bond consists of a pair of electrons shared between two adjacent atoms. The removal of two electrons and two hydrogen ions (H^+) from malate leaves four electrons to be shared between the carbon and oxygen atoms. This creates a carbon-oxygen double bond.

In most cases, the loss of an electron (e^-) is accompanied by the loss of a hydrogen ion, or proton (H^+). Similarly, when a molecule is reduced, it normally accepts a proton to balance the negative charge of the acquired electron and maintain electrical neutrality. Note, however, that NAD^+, because it starts out with a positive charge, accepts two electrons but only one proton. In this case, the second proton simply joins the pool of protons that normally exists in the aqueous cytoplasm.

Scientists measure the concentration of protons in an aqueous solution as the acidity or pH; the lower the pH value, the higher the concentration of protons. Can you think of some foods that have very low pH values?

ATP: WHAT IS IT AND HOW DOES IT WORK?

Adenosine triphosphate (ATP) is the principal means for moving energy around in the cell. ATP is a small molecule with three principal components: a nitrogenous base called **adenine**, a five-carbon sugar called **ribose**, and three phosphate groups (Figure 2.4). The adenine-ribose combination with a single phosphate group is the nucleotide called adenylic acid. You will recognize adenylic acid as one of the two nucleotides in NAD and NADP (see Figure 2.2). You may also remember this molecule as one of the four building blocks in DNA and RNA. The only difference is the absence of one oxygen atom on the ribose molecule in DNA, which makes it a deoxyribose sugar. Adenine itself is the letter "A" in the genetic code. Adenylic acid and related nucleotides clearly contain a lot of "information" that makes them useful to the cell in many different ways.

ATP is a lot like a rechargeable battery. It is charged with energy in the chloroplast or mitochondrion by adding a phosphate group to **adenosine diphosphate** (**ADP**). The energy of ATP is then tapped by transferring that same phosphate group from ATP to another molecule, which is a process called **phosphorylation**. The recipient might be a protein, a sugar, or almost any other kind of molecule. Indeed, the cell runs almost exclusively on phosporylated molecules and the principal source of phosphate groups is ATP. When a phosphate group is transferred from ATP, the energy associated with that phosphate group goes along with it and the leftover ADP molecule is available to be recharged. A metabolically active cell may require as many as several million ATP molecules every second. However, the cellular ATP/ADP pool is actually rather small, so ATP and ADP must turn over very rapidly.

ATP has been called a high-energy molecule and the phosphate bonds in ATP have been called high-energy bonds. However, these bonds are not particularly strong, so there is not an exceptionally high amount of energy available when these bonds

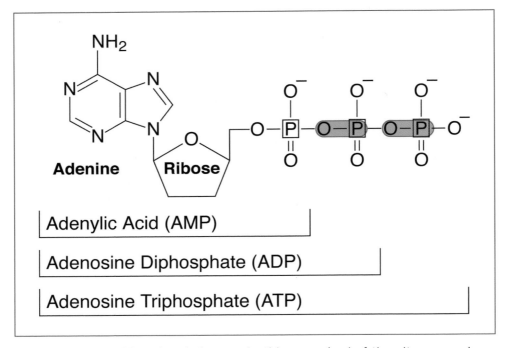

Figure 2.4 The ATP molecule is a nucleotide comprised of the nitrogenous base adenine, the five-carbon sugar ribose, and three phosphate groups. In most reactions, the terminal phosphate group is transferred, leaving a molecule of adenosine diphosphate (ADP). The two terminal phosphate bonds, however, are energetically equivalent and in some reactions they are transferred, leaving a molecule of adenylic acid (adenosine monophosphate or AMP).

are broken. The true value of ATP's role as an energy currency lies in the fact that its phosphate bond energies are neither high nor low, but intermediate in value. This enables ATP to assume the role of middle man, linking energy-rich molecules or reactions with other molecules or reactions that require energy. In some ways, ATP is a cellular Robin Hood, taking energy from the (energy) rich and giving it to the (energy) poor.

We will use the synthesis of glucose-1-phosphate, the precursor to starch synthesis, as an example to show how ATP works. Every chemical reaction is at least theoretically reversible and a reaction that is endergonic in one direction will be exergonic in the reverse. The difference in free energy (ΔG) between ATP and ADP + P_i, for example, is 30.5 kJ per mole. This means that the value of ΔG for the hydrolysis of ATP to ADP + P_i (the exergonic reaction) is 30.5 kJ per mole. The value of ΔG for the synthesis of ATP from ADP and P_i (the endergonic reaction) is +30.5 kJ per mole.

With the appropriate enzyme, the synthesis of ATP can be coupled to a reaction such as the hydrolysis of phospho-enolpyruvate. This reaction can happen because the free energy content of phosphoenolpyruvate is about twice that of ATP. The two half reactions are:

$$\text{Phosphoenolpyruvate} + H_2O \longrightarrow \text{pyruvate} + P_i$$
$$\Delta G = -61.9 \text{ kJ/mol}$$

and

$$\text{ADP} + P_i \longrightarrow \text{ATP} + H_2O$$
$$\Delta G = +30.5 \text{ kJ/mol}$$

Adding these two half reactions, we get the overall coupled reaction, which is:

$$\text{Phosphoenolpyruvate} + \text{ADP} \longrightarrow \text{pyruvate} + \text{ATP}$$
$$\Delta G = -31.4 \text{ kJ/mol}$$

Note that the sum of the free energy changes for the coupled reaction is still negative. As long as ΔG for the overall coupled reaction is negative (i.e., exergonic), the reaction will proceed spontaneously.

Now the ATP can move to some other location in the cell where glucose-1-phosphate is needed as a precursor for starch synthesis. The energy for starch synthesis is transferred from ATP to glucose through another set of coupled reactions:

$$ATP + H_2O \longrightarrow ADP + P_i \qquad\qquad \Delta G = -30.5 \text{ kJ/mol}$$

$$Glucose + P_i \longrightarrow Glucose\text{-}1\text{-}P + H_2O \qquad\qquad \Delta G = +20.9 \text{ kJ/mol}$$

$$ATP + Glucose \longrightarrow Glucose\text{-}1\text{-}phosphate + ADP \quad \Delta G = -8.6 \text{ kJ/mol}$$

Again, this enzyme-coupled reaction is energetically favorable because the net free energy change is still negative (exergonic).

The overall result is that ATP has functioned as a courier by carrying some of the free energy of the phosphoenolpyruvate molecule to another location in the cell where the energy was used to make glucose-1-phosphate. The phosphorylated glucose is now ready to be added to an elongating starch molecule. Meanwhile, the ADP returns to be recharged with another phosphate group.

A look at the numbers in the above reactions will reveal that, for this particular set of reactions, a substantial amount of energy has been "lost." We started out with a free energy of almost 62 kJ (14.8 kcal) and conserved only 8.6 kJ (2.1 kcal) in the glucose-1-phosphate. The "lost" energy, 53.4 kJ (12.7 kcal), has been dissipated as heat within the environment of the cell, a further contribution to the ever increasing entropy of the universe.

Summary

Life runs on solar power. A small portion of the light generated in the sun by hydrogen fusion reactions is captured by plants, but that is sufficient to run virtually the entire biosphere. The science that studies the capture of solar energy by plants and its flow through the biosphere is called bioenergetics. Every stage of energy flow from the sun to plants to animals is governed by two simple thermodynamic laws. The first and second laws of thermodynamics tell us that (1) the energy of the universe is constant; and (2) as energy flows through the system, the amount of free energy available to do work steadily diminishes.

The two most common methods for transferring energy between molecules are oxidation-reduction reactions and the exchange of phosphate groups mediated by ATP, commonly referred to as the energy currency of the cell. Oxidation-reduction reactions involve an exchange of electrons and, sometimes, accompanying protons between electron donors and electron acceptors. A loss of electrons is called oxidation and a gain of electrons is called reduction. Both photosynthesis and respiration are oxidation-reduction reactions.

In photosynthesis, electrons extracted from water are energized using the free energy of sunlight to produce a strong reducing agent, NADPH, which is subsequently used to reduce carbon dioxide to sugar. In respiration, sugar is re-oxidized and the free energy released on oxidation is used to generate ATP from ADP and inorganic phosphate. ATP is essentially an energy broker: it transfers free energy from energy-rich molecules to molecules that require the energy for the synthesis of larger molecules or other work in the cell.

He had been eight years upon a project for extracting
sunbeams out of cucumbers, which were to be put in vials,
hermetically sealed, and let out to warm the air in raw, inclement summers.

—Jonathan Swift
"A Voyage to Laputa"

Photosynthesis:
Light-Dependent Reactions

THE DUAL NATURE OF LIGHT

Light is a form of energy; a part of the electromagnetic spectrum along with radio waves, microwaves, infrared and ultraviolet radiation, X rays, gamma rays, and cosmic rays. Light, along with the rest of the electromagnetic spectrum, is a peculiar form of energy because it can be described in two ways. Depending on the situation, it can behave either as a wave or as a particle of energy.

More than 300 years ago, the English physicist Sir Isaac Newton conducted a simple experiment showing that a narrow beam of sunlight could be separated into a spectrum of different colors by passing it through a prism (Figure 3.1). But it was not until the late 19th century that James Maxwell demonstrated that light travels through space in continuous waves, like the ripples that spread out when a stone is dropped into a pond. Waves are characterized by their **wavelength**, or the distance from the peak of one wave to the peak of the next. Wavelengths of electromagnetic radiation vary from the very short wavelengths of cosmic rays (less than 0.1 nanometer, or nm) to very long radio waves (measured in thousands of meters). Visible light constitutes a very small portion of the spectrum, with wavelengths between 380 nm and 750 nm ($1 \text{ nm} = 10^{-9}$ meter).

Newton's experiment with the prism can be explained because light bends when it passes from one transparent substance to another, from air into a quartz prism, for example. This bending is referred to as **refraction** and the extent to which it bends is affected by wavelength. Shorter wavelengths are refracted more than longer wavelengths. Since each wavelength of light has a different color—the shortest wavelength is violet and the longest is called far-red—the light that emerges is separated into its component colors. The same phenomenon occurs when light is refracted by moisture drops in the air and the arc of a rainbow appears on the horizon.

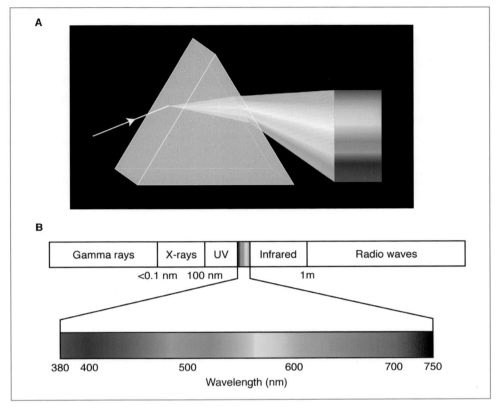

Figure 3.1 (A) Each time light passes from one medium to another, such as from air to a quartz prism, it bends or is refracted. Shorter wavelengths (violet) bend more sharply than longer wavelengths (red). (B) Light is that region of the electromagnetic spectrum with wavelengths between 380 nm and 750 nm.

Can you see any other examples of refraction in your environment?

The wave theory of light does not, however, fully explain the behavior of light. When light is emitted from an object (the tungsten filament in a light bulb, for example) or absorbed by a pigmented object, it behaves as though it is packaged in discrete particles of energy. The particle nature of light became evident around the turn of the 20th century, when it was shown that both ultraviolet radiation and light could dislodge electrons from metals such as zinc, sodium, or selenium. In order to account for this phenomenon, Albert Einstein proposed that electro-magnetic radiation was composed of packets of energy, which he called quanta (singular, **quantum**). A quantum of visible light is called a **photon**. The energy content of a photon is inversely pro-portional to its wavelength; that is, photons of short wavelength light contain more energy than photons of long wavelength light. For example, a photon of blue light, with a wavelength of 435 nm, has 1.5 times the energy of a photon of red light, with a wave-length of 660 nm.

Although visible light comprises only a very small portion of the electromagnetic spectrum, this limited range of wavelengths is responsible for a host of biological responses, such as vision, photosynthesis, **phototropism** (bending toward or away from the light), **photoperiodism** (the response of an organism to seasonal changes), and others. Why has life become so dependent on such a limited portion of the electromagnetic spectrum? One reason is simply because that is what is available to the biosphere. Most of the shorter wavelengths, such as the ultraviolet, are mostly filtered out by ozone and oxygen in the atmosphere. Longer wavelengths, such as infrared, are similarly filtered out by water vapor and carbon dioxide.

A second reason is that life is dependent upon proteins, nucleic acids, and other large molecules whose complicated structures are held together by relatively weak chemical bonds. Radiation with wavelengths shorter than violet light, such as ultraviolet and gamma rays, has sufficient energy to break these bonds and cause irreversible damage to the structure and function of these molecules. At the other end, the low energy content of infrared radiation can do little more than increase the thermal motion, or temperature, of molecules. Only radiation in the range of visible light has an energy level sufficient to induce subtle and biochemically useful changes in molecules without damaging them.

LIGHT AND PIGMENTS

A fundamental principle of photochemistry—photosynthesis is partly a photochemical reaction—is that for light to drive a reaction, it must first be absorbed. This means there must be a **pigment**, which is any molecule that absorbs light. A pigment that absorbs all wavelengths of light with equal efficiency will appear black. Most pigments, however, selectively absorb only

What Is Light?

Energy is an elusive quantity that cannot be seen, yet light is a form of energy that can be seen. Does that make light different from other forms of energy? Not at all.

Light is the portion of the electromagnetic spectrum with wavelengths between 380 nm and 750 nm. Radiation beyond 750 nm up to about 1 m is called infrared. We cannot see infrared radiation, but we can sense it because it warms our environment as it increases the motion of molecules. Radiation shorter than 380 nm but longer than 100 nm is called ultraviolet. We can't see ultraviolet, although it contains sufficient energy to cause serious damage to our cells if we get too much of it.

The human eye has a visual pigment called cis-retinal. When cis-retinal absorbs a photon of light, the energy of the photon causes the pigment to change its shape, which initiates a chain of events causing a nerve impulse to be sent to the brain. We cannot see infrared radiation because the energy of its photons is too low to induce the necessary change in cis-retinal. We also cannot see ultraviolet radiation because it is filtered out by the lens of the eye. This is just as well, for if ultraviolet radiation were to pass through the lens, the high energy level of its photons would likely damage the visual pigment.

Light is therefore nothing more than a physiological sensation. It is limited to the range of wavelengths with sufficient energy to change the shape of the visual pigment and stimulate the physiological sensation of vision in the human eye.

certain wavelengths, leaving the remaining wavelengths to be either transmitted or reflected. The transmitted or reflected light is what gives a pigment its characteristic color. The green color of leaves, for example, is due to the photosynthetic pigment chlorophyll (Figure 3.2). Chlorophyll appears green to the eye because it absorbs primarily the blue and red light at either end of the visible spectrum, leaving primarily green light from the middle of the spectrum to be transmitted or reflected.

With an instrument called a spectrophotometer, it is possible to measure how much of each wavelength of light is absorbed by a sample of pigment. The resulting graph is called an **absorption spectrum** (Figure 3.3). An absorption spectrum is an extremely useful tool because it is essentially a molecular fingerprint for a pigment. Every light-absorbing molecule has a characteristic absorption spectrum that is a key to its identification. For example, there are four different species of chlorophyll (designated a, b, c, and d). Although the absorption spectrum is generally similar for all four species, and they are all described as green, the precise wavelength at which peak absorption occurs will differ for each one (see Figure 3.3).

The first event in photosynthesis is the absorption of light by chlorophyll, but what actually happens when a pigment absorbs light? Absorption of a photon is an extremely rapid event. Within one femtosecond (1 fs = 10^{-15} seconds), the energy of the photon is transferred to an electron belonging to one of the atoms in the polar head of the chlorophyll molecule. Remember that electrons surround the nucleus of an atom in discrete orbitals. The additional energy supplied by a photon is sufficient to overcome the normal attraction between the electron and the nucleus of the atom and move the electron out to the next electron orbital. Only a photon with the energy that exactly matches the difference in energy levels between the two electron orbitals can be absorbed, which is why only certain wavelengths of light can be absorbed by any given molecule.

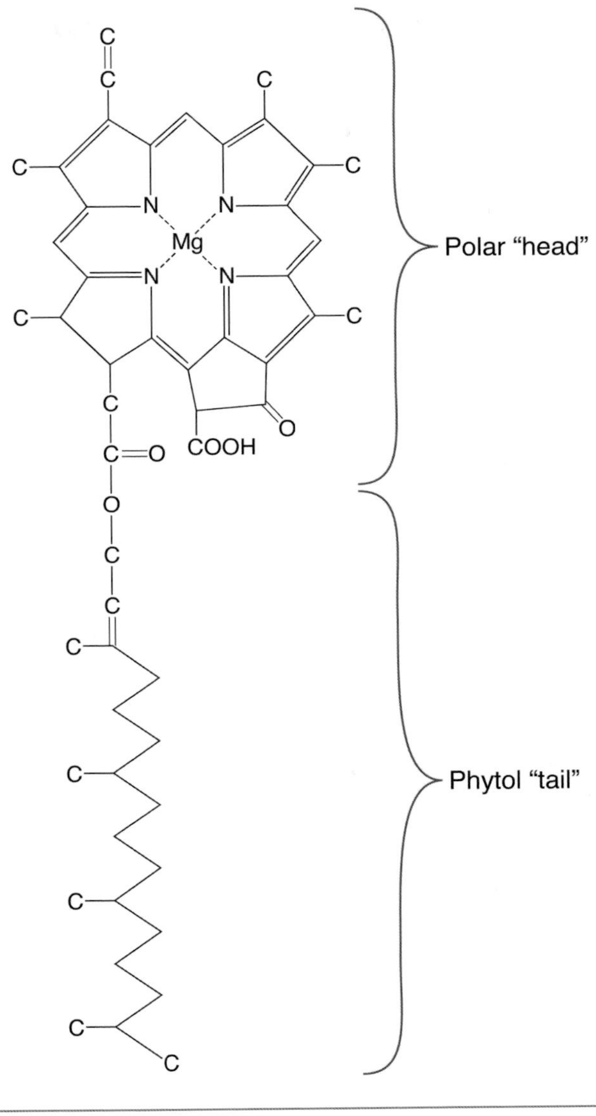

Figure 3.2 Chlorophyll consists of a polar head and a non-polar hydrocarbon tail. In this type of molecular representation, each intersection
of a line represents the position of a carbon atom. The polar head is
the portion of the molecule that absorbs photons. The non-polar hydrocarbon tail renders the molecule soluble in the lipid of the chloroplast
membrane.

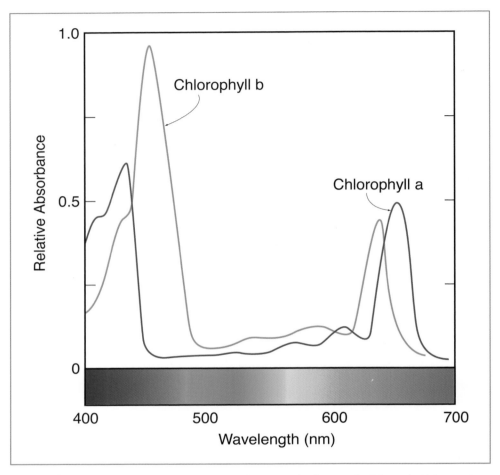

Figure 3.3 The absorption spectrum of chlorophyll a and chlorophyll b are two forms of chlorophyll found in higher plants. Each form absorbs strongly in the blue and red ends of the spectrum but the specific wavelengths of maximum absorption differ. An absorption spectrum can be used to identify various pigments.

A chlorophyll molecule that has absorbed a photon is said to be **excited.** The molecule contains more energy than it did when it was in the non-excited, **ground state.** An excited chlorophyll molecule is unstable and very short-lived—it has only a small fraction of a second in which to do something with that extra energy and return the molecule to the ground state. There are three things that can be done with this extra energy: (1) the energy may be dissipated as heat; (2) the energy may be re-emitted as light (a phenomenon known as **fluorescence**); or (3) the energy may be passed on to another molecule in a photo-chemical reaction. In the first two cases, the electron simply returns to its original orbital. In the latter case, the electron is transferred from the chlorophyll to another molecule, carrying the energy with it.

Chlorophyll is not the only pigment found in chloroplasts. There is also a family of orange and yellow pigments called **carotenoids**. Carotenoids include the **carotenes**, which are orange, and the **xanthophylls**, which are yellow. The principal carotene in chloroplasts is **beta-carotene**, which is located in the chloroplasts along with chlorophyll. At one time, the carotenoids were con-sidered accessory pigments—it was believed that light energy absorbed by carotenoids was transferred to the chlorophylls for use in photosynthesis. It now appears that carotenoids have little direct role in photosynthesis, but function largely to screen the chlorophylls from damage by excess light (see Chapter 6).

Carotenoid pigments are not limited to leaves, but are widespread in plant tissues. The color of carrot roots, for example, is due to high concentrations of beta-carotene in the root cells and **lycopene**, the red-orange pigment of tomatoes, is also a member of the carotenoid family. Lycopene and beta-carotene are important because of their purported health benefits. Beta-carotene from plants is also the principal source of vitamin A, which plays an important role in human vision. Lycopene is an antioxidant that may help protect against a variety of cancers.

Carotenes and xanthophylls are also responsible for the orange and yellow colors in autumn leaves. In response to short-ening day length and cooler temperatures, the chloroplast pig-ments begins to break down. Chlorophyll, which normally masks the carotenoids, breaks down more rapidly than the carotenoids and the carotenoids are revealed in their entire autumn splendor. The red color that appears in some leaves at this time of the year is due to water-soluble **anthocyanins**, whose synthesis is promoted by the same conditions that promote the breakdown of chlorophyll.

Where's the Chlorophyll?

If you are aware of plants in your environment, you will have noticed a large number of herbaceous plants, shrubs, and trees with leaves that are colored deep red or purple. Are these "green" plants? Is their photosynthesis any different?

Red leaves have the same palisade and spongy mesophyll cells as any green leaf. Chloroplasts in the mesophyll cells contain chlorophyll and carotenoids. To understand the difference between "green" leaves and "red" leaves, you must take a closer look at the leaf epidermal cells, because that is where the red pigments are found.

The deep red and purple colors are due to a class of pigments called anthocyanins. Anthocyanins are also responsible for the red, blue, and purple colors of flower petals. Chlorophyll and carotenoids are fat-soluble pigments that are located within the thylakoid membranes. This is why the water doesn't turn green when you boil green vegetables. If you boil red cabbage, however, the water will turn purple because anthocyanins are water-soluble pigments. In leaves, anthocyanins are found only in the vacuoles of epidermal cells, where they hide chlorophyll in the underlying mesophyll cells.

While the presence of anthocyanins may prevent you from seeing green chlorophyll in the middle of a leaf, they do not interfere with photosynthesis. This is because anthocyanins absorb principally green and yellow light from the middle of the spectrum and allow the red and blue portions of the spectrum, absorbed by chlorophyll, to pass unhindered through the epidermal cells.

Wild carrot (*Daucus caròta*, or Queen Anne's Lace) does not have highly pigmented roots. Can you suggest why the carrot we grow as a vegetable accumulates so much carotenoid pigment?

PHOTOSYSTEMS AND REACTION CENTERS

Chlorophyll and beta-carotene are localized in the thylakoid membranes, but not as individual, randomly distributed molecules. They are instead organized into large, multimolecular complexes called **photosystems** (or photosynthetic units). A photosystem is analogous to a satellite dish that collects a weak signal from space and focuses it on a sensor, which then feeds the signal to a receiver. A photosystem consists of several hundred chlorophyll molecules and associated proteins, most of which function as **antenna pigments** (Figure 3.4). When an antenna chlorophyll absorbs a photon, the excitation energy is passed to the next adjacent molecule and then to the next and so forth, until it eventually reaches the **reaction center.**

Each time the energy is transferred to another molecule, a small amount of energy is "lost" as heat (remember that no energy transfer is 100% efficient). This means that each successive chlorophyll molecule in the chain effectively absorbs a lower energy photon or longer wavelength of light. The energy is directed toward the reaction center because the chlorophyll there is the lowest energy level, longest wavelength form of chlorophyll in the photosystem. In other words, the excitation energy ends up at the reaction center because the reaction center chlorophyll is an energy "sink." Still, the transfer of excitation energy through a photosystem is efficient by most standards: on average, no more than 10% of the energy is lost.

The reaction center is where the actual conversion of light energy to chemical energy takes place. It consists of a unique chlorophyll molecule together with an electron acceptor and the enzymes necessary to extract electrons from water. When the energy of the absorbed photon reaches the reaction center,

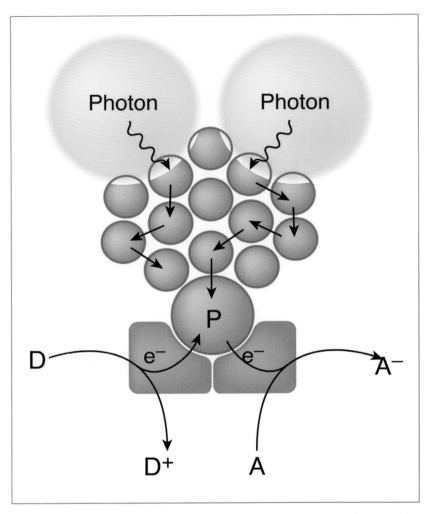

Figure 3.4 A photosystem may be viewed as an energy funnel: the energy of absorbed photons is passed from one chlorophyll molecule to the next until it reaches the reaction center chlorophyll (P). The excited reaction center chlorophyll then donates its energized electron to an electron acceptor (A). The electron deficiency of the reaction center chlorophyll is satisfied by extracting an electron from a donor (D).

the excited reaction center chlorophyll molecule gives up its energized electron, donating it to the electron acceptor. This leaves the reaction center chlorophyll molecule deficient of one electron, which is replaced by extracting one from water. When the reaction center has been excited four times, four electrons have been extracted from two molecules of water and one oxygen molecule (O_2) is released.

A photosystem is a model of photochemical efficiency, because of the speed of photochemical events. Remember that absorption of a photon by chlorophyll is a very rapid event, measured in femtoseconds. Events at the reaction center are less rapid, but are still measured in a microsecond (10^{-6} s) timescale. Even in bright sunlight, it is unlikely that any individual chlorophyll molecule would be struck by a photon more than a few times every second. Thus, a reaction center relying on a single or even a few chlorophyll molecules to provide it with light energy would probably sit idle most of the time. The advantage offered by a photosystem is that while the reaction center is busy processing one photon, other photons have been intercepted by the antenna molecules and are being funneled toward the reaction center. This arrangement ensures that as soon as the reaction center is free, additional excitation energy is immediately available and photosynthesis can proceed at its maximum rate. The result is that on a bright summer day, the reaction centers over a single square centimeter of leaf surface may process as many as 10^{19} photons.

THE PHOTOSYNTHETIC ELECTRON TRANSPORT CHAIN

Chloroplasts contain two different photosynthetic units, called photosystem I (PSI) and photosystem II (PSII). PSI and PSII operate in series, linked by a third protein complex called the **cytochrome complex**, to establish a photosynthetic **electron transport chain** (Figure 3.5). **Cytochromes** are a family of proteins that contain a heme group, similar to the oxygen-carrying hemoglobin in blood (although cytochromes tend to be blue, not red, in color). The heme group in cytochromes contains an iron atom (Fe) that cycles between the ferrous ion (Fe^{2+}) and ferric ion

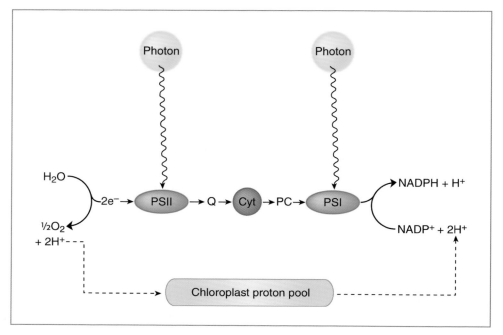

Figure 3.5 The linear representation of the photosynthetic electron transport chain shows that an electron extracted from water is passed through PSII and PSI to NADP. The electron gains energy as it passes through each photosystem, which provides sufficient energy to reduce $NADP^+$ to NADPH. Plastoquinone (Q), the cytochrome complex, and plastocyanin (PC) mediate the transfer of electrons between PSII and PSI. When water is oxidized, two protons (H^+) are released into the general pool of protons in the chloroplast. When $NADP^+$ is reduced at the other end, the necessary protons are withdrawn from the same pool.

(Fe^{3+}) as it is alternately reduced and oxidized. The overall effect of the electron transport chain is to extract low-energy electrons from water and, using light energy, raise their energy level sufficient to reduce $NADP^+$ (Figure 3.6). The resulting NADPH has a reducing potential sufficient to reduce carbon dioxide.

The flow of electrons through the electron transport chain begins with the absorption of a photon by an antenna chlorophyll molecule in PSII. The excitation energy migrates through adjacent antenna chlorophyll molecules until it reaches the reaction center, designated P680. The excited P680 transfers an electron to

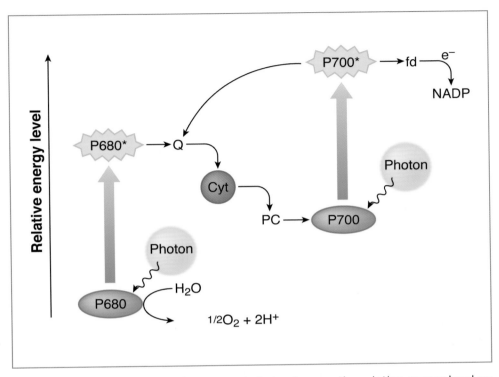

Figure 3.6 The photosynthetic transport chain changes the relative energy level as electrons pass through the chain. P680 and P700 represent the reaction center chlorophylls of PSII and PSI. P680* and P700* represent the excited reaction center chlorophylls. Both cyclic and non-cyclic electron transports are shown.

an electron acceptor called **pheophytin** (**Pheo**). This transfer leaves the reaction center chlorophyll deficient of one electron; it has been **photooxidized** ($P680^+$). Pheophytin, on the other hand, has gained one electron, so it has been reduced ($Pheo^-$).

The photooxidation of the PSII reaction center chlorophyll may seem like a small thing, but it is a most significant event for biology. Just as the separation of positive and negative poles in a storage battery represents potential chemical energy, the separation of a positive and negative charge between $P680^+$ and $Pheo^-$ represents the actual conversion of light energy to chemical energy in photosynthesis.

The balance of the electron transport chain simply ensures that this charge separation is stabilized and the energy is converted to more portable forms. The next thing that happens is that the electron lost from P680 when it was photooxidized is replaced by an electron from water, thus returning the reaction center chlorophyll to its ground state and preparing it to receive another incoming photon. At the same time, Pheo⁻ has quickly passed its energized electron to the cytochrome complex and is ready to accept another electron from the reaction center chlorophyll.

While all this has been going on in PSII, another photon has been received by photosystem I and its energy funneled to the PSI reaction center, designated P700. Another charge separation occurs as P700 is photooxidized and a small iron-protein called **ferredoxin** is reduced. The electron deficiency in P700 is satisfied by withdrawing an electron from the cytochrome complex and ferredoxin uses its electron to reduce NADP to NADPH.

The combined energy of two photons, exciting PSII and PSI, is more than is needed to reduce a molecule of NADP to NADPH. The chloroplasts use some of this spare energy to synthesize ATP, which is also required for the carbon fixation reactions.

MAKING ATP WITH PHOTONS

In the previous chapter, we illustrated one way of making ATP. That was an example of **substrate-level phosphorylation**, in which ATP is synthesized directly from another phosphorylated molecule. Substrate level phosphorylation, however, accounts for only a small portion of the ATP synthesized by cells. The bulk of the ATP is synthesized in the chloroplasts and mitochondria by an enzyme called **ATP synthetase (ATPase)**. The mechanism by which ATPase couples ATP synthesis with electron transport was first proposed by Peter Mitchell in 1961. Known as the **chemiosmotic coupling**, Mitchell's proposal provided the key to understanding cellular bioenergetics and for this significant contribution Mitchell was awarded the Nobel Prize in 1978.

ATP synthetase is a large complex located in the thylakoid membrane but separate from the two photosystems. The cytochrome complex that transfers electrons between PSII and PSI is a **transmembrane protein** that extends through the membrane into the aqueous medium of both the lumen and the stroma. When it is transferring electrons from PSII to PSI, the cytochrome complex also functions as a **proton pump.** As electrons flow through the complex, some of the free energy is used to move protons from the stroma into the lumen (Figure 3.7). This establishes an unequal distribution of protons, or proton gradient, across the membrane. The oxygen evolving complex of PSII is located on the lumen side of the thylakoid membrane, so the protons generated when water is split further add to the magnitude of this proton gradient.

Herbicides Inhibit Photosynthetic Electron Transport

Several common herbicides kill plants by interfering with photosynthetic electron transport. Triazine herbicides, including atrazine and simizine, are taken up by the roots and transported to the leaves, where they bind to a critical PSII reaction center protein. This binding blocks the transfer of electrons out of the reaction center and prevents the formation of both ATP and NADPH in the chloroplast.

The triazines are commonly used to control weeds in cornfields because corn roots contain an enzyme that degrades the herbicide and renders it inactive. Unfortunately, resistance to triazine herbicides has developed in many weed species. In most cases, resistance has been traced to a single amino acid change in one of the reaction center proteins. This change appears to prevent the triazine molecule from binding but does not interfere with electron transport. Continued application of the herbicide tends to increase the resistance in weeds.

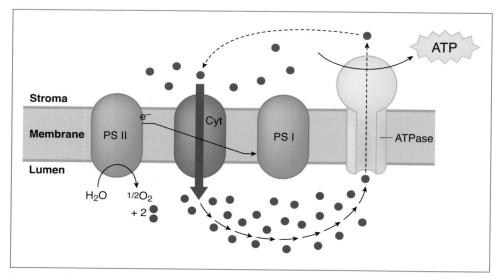

Figure 3.7 As electrons pass through the cytochrome complex (Cyt) on their way from PSII to PSI, the cytochrome complex pumps protons (small spheres) across the thylakoid membrane from the stroma into the lumen. This establishes a proton gradient that drives the synthesis of ATP when the protons pass back through the enzyme ATP synthetase (ATPase).

In bright sunlight, the difference in proton concentration across the thylakoid membrane can be as much as ten-fold, or a full pH unit. Since each proton is positively charged, the proton gradient also contributes to a difference in electrical potential across the membrane—a gradient of one pH unit is equivalent to −60 millivolts (mV). Together, the proton gradient and potential difference constitute a **proton motive force** equivalent to −180 mV (equivalent to 3 pH units) across the membrane, with the stroma being negative relative to the lumen. It takes a lot of energy to pump positively charged protons against such a proton motive force, energy that is provided by the electrons as they move energetically downhill between PSII and PSI.

As energy is required to establish the proton gradient in the first place (proton pumping is an endergonic process), the gradient represents stored free energy that can be harnessed to do work as the protons return to the stroma (an exergonic process). The proton motive force favors the return of the protons to the stroma because positively charged protons would normally be expected to diffuse from a region of high concentration to a region of low concentration and toward a negative charge. The problem is that the thylakoid membrane is made almost entirely of uncharged lipid (fat) molecules, which gives it the property of an electrical insulator. The charged protons can not return to the stroma by simple diffusion through the membrane because the membrane properties won't allow it.

This is where ATP synthetase is important. ATP synthetase is shaped like a lollipop (see Figure 3.7) and the "stick" of the lollipop, which extends across the membrane, provides a channel through which protons may return to the stroma. But they have to earn their passage: as they return to the stroma, the protons give up their energy so that the "head" of the lollipop can use it to make ATP from ADP and inorganic phosphate (P_i). The result is a continuous circuit of protons, with electron transport pumping protons from the stroma into the lumen and the protons generating ATP as they return to the stroma.

CYCLIC AND NON-CYCLIC PHOTOPHOSPHORYLATION

The situation in which electrons are extracted from water, flow through PSII and PSI, and are withdrawn as NADPH, is known as **non-cyclic electron transport** (see Figure 3.6). When ATP is formed as a consequence of non-cyclic electron transport, it is called **non-cyclic photophosphorylation**. Non-cyclic electron transport and photophosphorylation provide both the NADPH and ATP necessary for reducing carbon in the light-independent reactions.

Photosystem I may also operate independently of photosystem II. In this case, ferredoxin returns its electron to the cytochrome complex rather than to NADP. In effect, the same electrons are continuously cycled through photosystem I. Of course, no NADPH is formed, but ATP can still be generated as the electrons pass through the cytochrome complex. This type of electron flow is called **cyclic electron transport**, and ATP synthesis supported by cyclic electron transport is known as **cyclic photophosphorylation**. Cyclic photophosphorylation provides more ATP than required for carbon fixation alone. This additional ATP is used for other chloroplast activities, such as starch synthesis and active transport of solutes across the chloroplast membranes.

Summary

When traveling through space, light behaves as a wave, but when emitted or absorbed, light behaves as a particle. A particle of electromagnetic radiation is called a quantum; a quantum of visible light is called a photon.

Light is absorbed by pigments, each of which is characterized by a unique absorption spectrum. The color of a pigment is determined by the portion of the spectrum that it does not absorb. When a photon is absorbed, its energy is transferred to an electron in the pigment. Chlorophyll in the thylakoid membranes is organized along with specific proteins as multimolecular complexes called photosystems. Most of the photosystem is comprised of antenna chlorophylls that absorb photons and pass the energy on to the reaction center. At the reaction center, the actual conversion of light energy to chemical energy takes place.

Chloroplasts contain two photosystems that are linked in series to form an electron transport chain. During photosynthesis, the effect of the electron transport chain is to extract electrons from water and, using absorbed photons, elevate them energetically to the point where they can reduce NAD^+. The resulting NADH has sufficient reducing potential to reduce carbon dioxide to sugar.

The carbon fixation reactions require ATP as well as NADPH. The necessary ATP is synthesized in the chloroplasts by a mechanism known as chemiosmotic coupling. In addition to transporting electrons, the cytochrome complex that lies between PSII and PSI also functions as a proton pump. Pumping protons into the thylakoid lumen establishes a proton gradient and potential difference across the thylakoid membrane. Protons can return to the stroma only through the proton channel provided by ATP synthetase. In the process, the free energy stored in the proton gradient is used to drive the synthesis of ATP from ADP and inorganic phosphate. Because this ATP is synthesized during the light reactions, it is called photophosphorylation.

*Life exists in the universe only because
the carbon atom possesses certain exceptional properties.*

—James Jeans (1877—1946)
English Mathematician, astronomer

Photosynthesis:
Fixing Carbon

DISCOVERY

The metabolic pathways for fixing carbon dioxide were once referred to as the "dark reactions," but are now more commonly referred to as the **photosynthetic carbon reduction cycle**. It is also referred to as the **Calvin Cycle** after Melvin Calvin, who directed the research team that worked out the pathway in the 1950s. For this work, Calvin was awarded the Nobel Prize in 1961.

Calvin began his studies with a very straightforward objective—identify the first stable organic product that contains the carbon dioxide taken in by a plant. In order to accomplish this objective, Calvin had to resolve three problems. First, he had to have a way of marking, or labeling, the carbon dioxide taken up during photosynthesis so that its carbon atom could be distinguished from all the other carbon in the cell. Second, because the reactions involved were presumed to be enzymatic and therefore very rapid, he had to devise a system in which photosynthesis could be stopped after a very short period of time in the presence of the labeled carbon dioxide. This was necessary in order to trap the labeled carbon before it had become incorporated into too many sugars and other products. The third thing Calvin needed was a way to isolate and separate all the sugars and other small molecules and determine which molecules contained the labeled carbon. Calvin's overall objective was, then, to identify the molecule that contained the highest amount of label after the shortest possible exposure.

The problem of labeling the carbon dioxide was resolved by the discovery of the radioactive carbon **isotope** ^{14}C (pronounced C-fourteen), which became available in the late 1940s. Carbon dioxide labeled with ^{14}C can be followed by a variety of methods used to detect radioactive chemicals and is easily distinguished from non-radioactive carbon isotope ^{12}C (C-twelve). To resolve the second problem, Calvin devised a system using the unicellular green alga *Chlorella*, whose photosynthesis is the same as higher plants. Calvin grew the *Chlorella* in a glass vessel that was

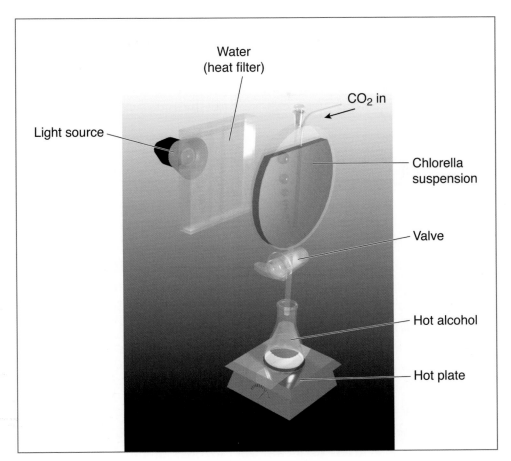

Figure 4.1 The lollipop apparatus was used by Melvin Calvin to study the path of carbon in photosynthesis. The experiment began when a small volume of carbon dioxide containing radioactive carbon-14 ($^{14}CO_2$) was injected into the carbon dioxide stream. The valve was immediately opened, allowing the *Chlorella* suspension to drain into the hot alcohol below. The hot alcohol stopped any further reactions and extracted the sugars from the cells. With this arrangement, the time of exposure to $^{14}CO_2$ could be limited to a few seconds.

shaped something like a lollipop (Figure 4.1). With the lights on and the algae actively photosynthesizing, $^{14}CO_2$ was injected into the culture vessel. Almost immediately, the valve was opened, allowing the algal suspension to fall into a beaker of hot alcohol. The hot alcohol actually fulfilled two functions.

First, the hot alcohol immediately denatured all the proteins and stopped any further enzymatic reactions. Second, the hot alcohol extracted the sugars and other small molecules for subsequent analysis. Using this simple but highly effective system, Calvin was able to limit exposure to the radioactive carbon

Paper Chromatography and Autoradiography

In paper chromatography, a concentrated extract containing a complex mixture of sugars or other compounds is applied to a spot on a sheet of filter paper. Once dry, the edge of the paper is lowered into a tray of organic solvent. The solvent slowly moves up the paper, while different molecular species migrate at different rates and separate from each other. When the solvent reaches the top of the paper, the sheet is removed from the solvent and dried. The final product is called a **chromatogram**.

When the experiment is repeated under the same conditions and with the same solvent mixture, any chemical compound, such as in Calvin's experiments, will always migrate to the same position relative to the solvent front. If the distance moved by the compound in question is divided by the distance moved by the solvent, the result is a ratio called the R_F. R_F values are also used to locate and identify unknown compounds. Molecules that contain small amounts of radioactivity can then be located on a chromatogram by a technique known as **autoradiography**. In autoradiography, the chromatogram is placed against a sheet of X-ray film in the dark for a predetermined period of time. The radioactivity exposes the film, creating dark spots on the film when it is developed. The corresponding radioactive compound can then be extracted from the chromatogram paper, chemically identified, and measured by Geiger counters or similar instruments. The sugars can even be systematically and chemically broken down by chemical means so that one can determine which carbon in the sugar actually carries the label.

dioxide to periods measured in a few seconds. The third problem of separating the sugars and other small molecules and identifying which contained the labeled carbon, was resolved by using the then new techniques of **paper chromatography** and **autoradiography.**

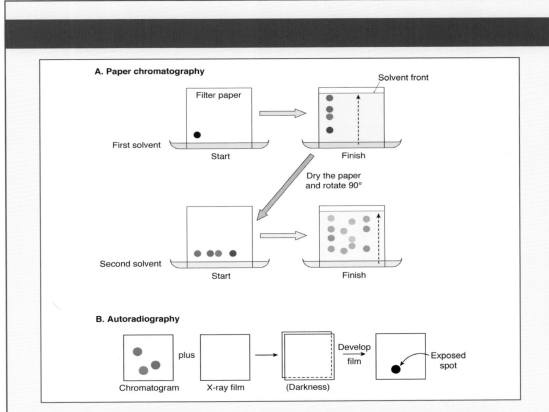

(A.) A mixture of compounds or plant extract is "spotted" near the corner of a filter paper square. The edge of the paper is then placed in a solvent which slowly migrates up the paper, carrying the chemicals with it. Different chemicals in the spot will separate because they migrate at different rates. When the solvent reaches the top of the paper, the paper is removed from the solvent, dried, and turned 90°. The process is repeated with a second solvent. (B.) Radioactive chemicals on the paper can be located by exposing the finished chromatogram to a sheet of X-ray film.

Using this combination of techniques, Calvin found that when photosynthesis in the presence of the radioactive carbon dioxide was limited to two seconds, most of the radioactivity was associated with a three-carbon organic acid called **3-phosphoglyceric acid (PGA)**. PGA was clearly the first stable product of photosynthesis, but that was only part of the answer. How was a three-carbon molecule formed from carbon dioxide, which contains only one carbon? The most logical possibility was that the carbon dioxide was added to a two-carbon molecule, but no two-carbon molecules could be found. Then Calvin identified a five-carbon sugar called ribulose-1,5-bisphosphate (RuBP) as one of the molecules that quickly became labeled with radioactive carbon. RuBP was soon identified as the acceptor molecule. The fact that RuBP was an early labeled product indicated that it was regenerated from PGA and that there was a cycle involved.

Calvin and his co-workers went on to show how the carbon dioxide was incorporated into the PGA, how the PGA was converted into simple sugars, how these sugars were assembled into more complex carbohydrates, and how the RuBP was regenerated.

THE PATH OF CARBON IN PHOTOSYNTHESIS

The photosynthetic carbon reduction cycle, or PCR cycle, is divided into three stages, all of which take place in the chloroplast stroma. The first stage is the carboxylation reaction, in which one molecule of CO_2 is attached to the five-carbon sugar RuBP, yielding two molecules of PGA (Figure 4.2). This carboxylation reaction, so-called because the net effect is to add a carboxyl (–COOH) group to RuBP, is catalyzed by the enzyme ribulose-1,5-bisphosphate carboxylase (**Rubisco** for short). Rubisco, located in the chloroplast stroma, may comprise up to 50% of the total soluble protein in leaves. That is one reason that spinach and other

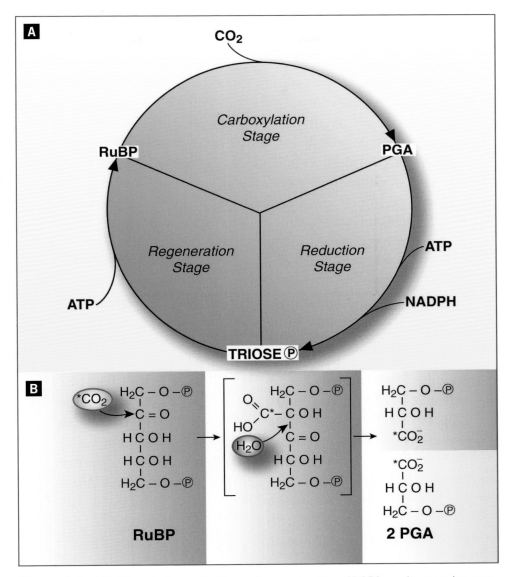

Figure 4.2 (A) The photosynthetic carbon reduction (PCR) cycle may be conveniently divided into three stages. (B) During the carboxylation stage of the PCR cycle, a molecule of carbon dioxide is condensed with a molecule of RuBP, forming a six-carbon intermediate. The intermediate exists only briefly as part of the enzyme-substrate complex. It is released from the enzyme as two molecules of phosphoglyceric acid (PGA). Only one molecule of PGA contains the newly incorporated carbon.

leafy green vegetables are so good for you—they are just loaded with Rubisco protein! How much Rubisco protein is included in your diet?

The carboxylation reaction is an exergonic, spontaneous reaction with a free energy change of about -35 kJ per mole. This means that carboxylation can occur without the need for any energy input. Indeed, if you mixed some RuBP, Rubisco, and appropriate cofactors together in a test tube, you could expect to see PGA synthesized in the dark. Of course the reaction in the test tube would not continue; it would grind to a halt as soon as the RuBP was used up. This is also what would happen in the chloroplast without the energy supplied by the light reactions. This energy is required to remove the PGA—and, of course, to make sugars—and also to regenerate RuBP. In other words, the energy of the light reactions is required to keep the cycle going by removing the product and regenerating the carbon dioxide acceptor.

The product of carbon fixation, PGA, is removed in the second or reduction stage of the PCR cycle in which PGA is chemically reduced to a three-carbon sugar called **glyceraldehyde-3-phosphate** (**G3P**). Reduction of PGA to G3P is an endergonic reaction that requires the energy of both ATP and NADPH. This is the first energy-requiring stage and is the stage from which the cycle derives its name, photosynthetic carbon *reduction* cycle.

$$PGA + ATP + NADPH \longrightarrow G3P + ADP + NAD^+ + P_i$$

The carbon dioxide acceptor RuBP is regenerated in the third stage of the PCR cycle (Figure 4.3). This stage is comprised of a number of reactions involving a pool of three-, four-, six-, and seven-carbon sugars. The idea is to start with three-carbon molecules—the products of the reduction stage—and end up with the five-carbon acceptor molecule. The

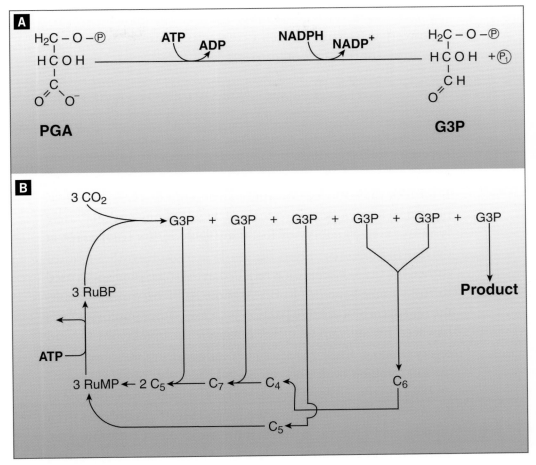

Figure 4.3 (A) During the reduction stage of the PCR cycle, both ATP and NADPH, products of the light reactions, are required to reduce PGA to glyceraldehyde-3-phosphate (G3P). In this reaction, the acid or carboxyl group (–COOH) of PGA is chemically reduced to an aldehyde group (–CHO) in G3P. (B) The regeneration stage of the PCR cycle is a series of sugar rearrangements. For example, two three-carbon sugars combine to form a six-carbon sugar.

net effect of these sugar rearrangements is to generate a molecule of ribulose-5-phosphate or ribulose monophosphate (RuMP), a five-carbon sugar essentially identical to RuBP except that it contains only one phosphate group instead of two. The missing phosphate is, of course, supplied by ATP in the final step of the regeneration stage. The result is that RuMP is converted to RuBP, which is ready to continue the cycle by accepting another carbon dioxide.

$$\text{G3P} \longrightarrow \text{sugar rearrangements} \longrightarrow \text{RuMP} + \text{ATP} \longrightarrow \text{RuBP} + \text{ADP}$$

While this may seem like a roundabout way of getting the RuBP necessary to keep carbon uptake going, regenerating RuBP from an existing pool of sugars is actually a more efficient use of resources than manufacturing a fresh supply every time it is needed to fix a carbon dioxide molecule. It also means that there is always a small supply of RuBP available in the chloroplast at dawn when photosynthesis begins. When photosynthesis is just turned on, the fixed carbon is retained in the sugar pool and is used to build up the supply of RuBP. As more RuBP becomes available, the rate of carbon dioxide fixation increases. Once photosynthesis has been brought up to speed, however, the uptake of CO_2 and regeneration of RuBP reach a steady state and any additional fixed carbon can then be drained off to make glucose.

Because the carbon dioxide enters the cycle one molecule at a time, it is necessary to turn the cycle six times in order to get a molecule of glucose, a six-carbon molecule. Combining six molecules of CO_2 with six molecules of RuBP yields 12 molecules of PGA. The 12 PGA molecules are then reduced to 12 molecules of G3P, using the energy from 12 molecules of ATP and 12 molecules of NADPH. Two of the 12 G3P molecules (six carbons) can be used to make one molecule of glucose (six carbons). The remaining ten G3P molecules (30 carbons) enter the sugar conversion part of the cycle to regenerate, at the cost of another six ATP, the original six RuBP (30 carbons).

PHOTORESPIRATION

Simultaneous with the assimilation of CO_2 through photosynthesis, CO_2 is also being released as a product of cellular respiration in the mitochondria of leaf cells and other cells. At about the same time that Calvin was working out the PCR cycle, however, independent studies demonstrated that a significant proportion of the CO_2 released by green plants did not originate in the mitochondria and its release was light-dependent. This light-dependent CO_2 release by plants is called **photorespiration**. Photorespiration and photosynthesis are clearly antagonistic processes. At the same time photosynthesis is using light energy to assimilate carbon dioxide, light energy is also being used to release some of that CO_2 back into the atmosphere.

This apparent contradiction arises because the carbon-fixing enzyme Rubisco is unable to discriminate between CO_2 and O_2 as a substrate. Both CO_2 and O_2 compete for the same active site on the enzyme and both produce product. The difference is that when Rubisco "fixes" oxygen, the products are one molecule of phosphoglycerate plus a two-carbon molecule called phospho-glycolate (Figure 4.4). The phosphoglycerate stays within the PCR cycle, but the phosphoglycolate is subsequently metabo-lized by two other organelles—the mitochondrion and the peroxisome—in a process that ultimately ends up with the release of carbon dioxide.

Photorespiration is a costly process for the plant (Figure 4.5). It has been estimated that in normal air, which is 21% oxygen, as much as one-third of the carbon assimilated through photo-synthesis is lost through photorespiration. In addition, the amount of ATP and reducing potential (NADH) expended in the metabolism of phosphoglycolate is greater than what is required to reduce a molecule of carbon dioxide, so it is logical to ask why a plant should indulge in such a wasteful process. This is not an easy question to answer and several possibilities have been put forward.

The most favored thesis is that photorespiration acts as a kind of safety valve for the light reactions when the supply of carbon

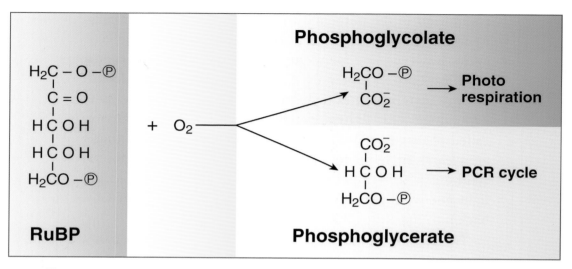

Figure 4.4 Photorespiration occurs when RuBP "fixes" a molecule of oxygen instead of carbon dioxide; the products are only one molecule of 3-phosphoglyceric acid plus one molecule of the two-carbon phosphoglycolate. The phosphoglycolate is transported to other organelles (the peroxisome and the mitochondrion), where a complex series of reactions results in its breakdown and the release of carbon dioxide.

dioxide is limited in strong light. For example, when plants are subjected to extreme moisture stress, the stomata will close to prevent further water loss from the leaves. But closed stomata also restrict the uptake of carbon dioxide. If Rubisco were limited to fixing only carbon dioxide, the plant would be unable to use the ATP and NADPH generated by the light reactions, forcing the electron transport system to shut down. Chlorophyll, however, would continue to be excited and, with no way to use the excitation energy, would very likely suffer photooxidative damage. Photorespiration provides a means to protect the system against photooxidative damage under these conditions. It could do this by consuming oxygen generated in the light reactions, thus providing an alternative use for ATP and NADPH and allowing the continued operation of the electron transport chain.

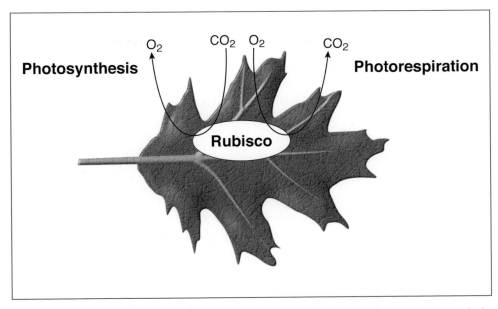

Figure 4.5 Photosynthesis and photorespiration are competing processes. It is believed that, under optimal conditions, photorespiration may return to the atmosphere as much as one-third of the carbon originally fixed by photosynthesis.

Scientists have long believed that it might be possible to improve crop productivity if photorespiration could be suppressed or genetically eliminated. Unfortunately, scientists have been singularly unsuccessful in this quest, but in the next section we will describe a group of plants that have done exactly that. These plants have a modified photosynthesis that suppresses photorespiratory carbon loss and improves the overall efficiency of carbon assimilation.

C₄ PHOTOSYNTHESIS

Although most plants assimilate carbon solely through the PCR cycle, there is a significant group of plants in which the first product of photosynthesis is not PGA. Working in Hawaii in the early 1960s, H. P. Korchack applied Calvin's method of rapid CO_2 fixation to sugarcane and reported that the first product was not PGA, as might be expected, but a four-carbon organic acid called oxaloacetic acid (OAA) instead. PGA did become labeled, but only later. In order to distinguish between these two types of photosynthesis, plants in which the three-carbon PGA is the first product are now identified as **C₃ plants**, while those in which the first product is a four-carbon organic acid are identified as **C₄ plants**. In addition to sugarcane, some of our most productive crop species, such as corn and sorghum, are C$_4$ plants.

C$_4$ plants exhibit a number of physiological and anatomical features that constitute what is commonly referred to as the C$_4$ syndrome. One of the most important distinctions between C$_3$ and C$_4$ plants is the anatomical arrangement of the photosynthetic cells in the middle of their leaves (Figure 4.6). Recall that the mesophyll of a typical C$_3$ plant has both a palisade layer of tightly packed columnar cells and a spongy layer of irregular cells along with a network of air space (see Chapter 1). Carbon fixation and sugar synthesis takes place via the PCR cycle in both the palisade and the spongy mesophyll cells. In the leaves of C$_4$ plants, however, the leaf veins, or vascular bundles, are surrounded by a ring of tightly packed cells called the **bundle sheath**, which contain an especially large numbers of chloroplasts This distinctive arrangement of cells sheathing the vascular bundle is called **Kranz anatomy**, from the German word for "wreath." Between veins are the more loosely packed mesophyll cells, similar to the spongy mesophyll of C$_3$ plants. C$_4$ plants lack the distinctive palisade mesophyll cells so typical of C$_3$ plants.

The distinction between bundle sheath and mesophyll cells plays a key role in C$_4$ photosynthesis (Figure 4.7). The bundle sheath cells contain Rubisco and carry out carbon fixation using the PCR cycle, like any C$_3$ plant. The mesophyll cells, on the other hand, contain an enzyme called **phosphoenolpyruvate carboxylase (PEPcase)** that catalyzes the formation

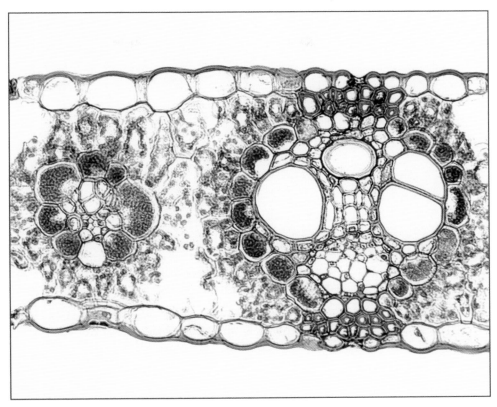

Figure 4.6 The unique aspect of leaves that use the C_4 photosynthetic cycle is the existence of the bundle sheath cells that completely encompass the leaf veins or vascular bundles.

of OAA from the three-carbon acid phosphoenolpyruvate and carbon dioxide.

$$\text{Phosphoenolpyruvate} + CO_2 \longrightarrow \text{oxaloacetate}$$

In the next step, oxaloacetic acid is reduced to malic acid, another four-carbon organic acid, which is immediately translocated from the mesophyll cell into an adjacent bundle sheath cell. Once inside the bundle sheath cell, the initial carboxylation reaction is reversed. Malic acid is decarboxylated,

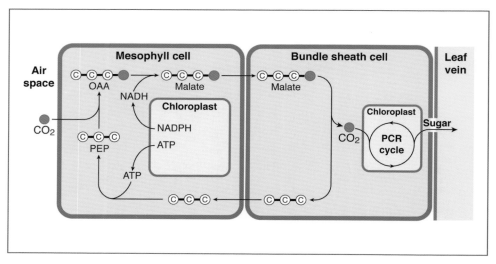

Figure 4.7 C_4 plants initially fix carbon as oxaloacetic acid (OAA) in the mesophyll cells. OAA is then reduced to malic acid (malate), which is transported into an adjacent bundle sheath cell where the malic acid is decarboxylated. CO_2 then enters the PCR cycle, while the remaining three-carbon acid returns to the mesophyll cells to continue the cycle. The C_4 cycle helps pump carbon dioxide into the bundle sheath cells, where high CO_2 concentration suppresses photorespiration.

giving up the carbon dioxide originally assimilated in the mesophyll cell and generating a C_3 acid. The carbon dioxide enters the PCR cycle and is incorporated into sugars. Meanwhile, the C_3 acid returns to the mesophyll cell where it is phosphorylated to regenerate phosphoenolpyruvate and complete the cycle.

If you compare the C_4 cycle with the C_3 cycle you will see that energy from the light reactions is required in essentially the same places in order to accomplish the same objectives. Reduction potential (as NADH or NADPH) is used to reduce the initial product (OAA versus PGA) and ATP is required to regenerate the acceptor molecule (PEP versus RuBP). The translocation of the product of C_4 carboxylation into the bundle sheath cell and its subsequent decarboxylation means that, unlike the C_3 cycle, the C_4 cycle itself does not actually result in any net carbon reduction. C_4 plants still ultimately rely on the operation of

Calvin's PCR cycle in the bundle sheath cells for the production of sugars.

Do these somewhat complicated anatomical and metabolic arrangements offer C_4 plants any advantage over C_3 plants? It appears they might, at least under certain circumstances. The C_4 cycle suppresses photorespiration and C_4 plants are able to

Crabgrass and Other C_4 Success Stories

Plants with C_4 photosynthesis evolved in tropical and subtropical regions and are well-adapted to conditions of high light, high temperature, and low moisture. Although C_4 species are now distributed throughout North America, they are most abundant in areas with high light, high temperature, or both during the growing season.

One example that plagues homeowners is crabgrass (*Digitaria sanguinales*). Most residential lawns, at least in the more temperate regions of North America, are planted with fine-leaved C_3 grasses such as Kentucky bluegrass (*Poa pratensis*) and bent grass (*Agrostis* spp.). Crabgrass is a spreading, yellow-green, broadleaved C_4 grass that often takes over lawns during the hot, dry months in the middle of summer. Under conditions when water is at a premium, the high transpiration ratio (or low water-use efficiency) of C_3 grasses means they are simply unable to compete with the more productive crabgrass.

Many of our most productive crop species are also C_4 species. These include corn or maize (*Zea mays*), millet (*Pennisetum typhoides*), sorghum (*Sorghum vulgare*), and sugar cane (*Saccharum officinarum*), all cultivated in the drier tropical climates found in Africa and Central America. The only exception is corn—through extensive hybridization over the past 60 years, the northern limits for growing corn have steadily advanced. However, much to the frustration of farmers, many of our more aggressive weeds, including Russian thistle (*Salsola kali*) and pigweed (*Amaranthus* spp.) are also C_4 species.

maintain higher rates of photosynthesis when the CO_2 supply is limited.

Let's look first at the photorespiration problem. The enzyme Rubisco found in the bundle sheath cells of C_4 plants is the same enzyme found in C_3 plants and consequently has the same potential for carbon dioxide loss through photorespiration. Remember that carbon dioxide and oxygen compete for the active site on Rubisco, so any action that increases the ratio of carbon dioxide to oxygen will tend to limit photorespiration. The C_4 cycle, in fact, serves as a carbon dioxide pump that concentrates carbon dioxide in the bundle sheath cells. The higher concentration of carbon dioxide favors carboxylation of Rubisco over oxygenation and thus suppresses photorespiration. At the same time, any carbon dioxide that might chance to be released through photorespiration in the bundle sheath remains trapped within the leaf by the enzyme PEPcase in the surrounding mesophyll cells, where it is recycled into OAA and pumped back into the bundle sheath cells.

Because photorespiration is suppressed in C_4 plants, they are able to maintain higher rates of photosynthesis at lower carbon dioxide levels compared to C_3 plants. Such a situation might arise when the stomata are partially closed to conserve water during periods of water stress. Even moderate water stress will severely limit the uptake of carbon dioxide, which affects C_3 plants much more than it affects C_4 plants. One measure of this effect is called the transpiration ratio—the ratio of the amount of water transpired from the leaf to the amount of carbon dioxide assimilated. For C_3 plants, the transpiration ratio is typically in the range of 500 to 1,000, while for C_4 plants the values of 200 to 350 are normal. The much lower transpiration ratio means that C_4 plants are able to fix carbon even when the stomata are nearly closed. C_4 plants would thus appear to gain a photosynthetic advantage over C_3 plants in hotter, drier climates where moisture stress is more likely.

Crassulacean Acid Metabolism— Working the Night Shift

Another interesting variation in photosynthetic carbon fixation is known as Crassulacean Acid Metabolism, or CAM. Members of the family Crassulaceae, for which this particular form of metabolism was named, are **succulent plants** found in **xerophytic habitats**. Succulence means that they have thick, fleshy leaves (or in the case of the cacti, photosynthetic stems) and xerophytic means that the habitat is extremely dry, as in a desert. Like C_4 photosynthesis, CAM plants use the PEP carboxylase pathway as a CO_2 concentrating mechanism and the PCR cycle to fix the carbon. But where C_4 plants separate the PEP carboxylation and the PCR cycle spatially (between the mesophyll cells and bundle sheath cells), CAM plants separate them cyclically.

One of the most striking features of CAM plants is an inverted stomatal cycle—their stomata are open at night and closed during the day. This means that the photosynthetic factory in CAM plants works a double shift. During the night shift, CAM plants open the stomata and take in CO_2. Since there is no light available to drive photosynthesis, CAM plants have to store the CO_2 by forming four-carbon malic acid from CO_2 and phosphoenolpyruvate. The malic acid is then pumped into the cell's large central vacuole where it remains until dawn. During the day shift, when the energy to convert carbon into sugars is available, the malic acid returns to the cytoplasm where it is decarboxylated and the CO_2 is taken up by the chloroplasts, where it enters the PCR cycle.

CAM thus allows plants to take in carbon dioxide during the night when stomata can be opened with reduced risk of water loss. These nocturnal plants can then fix the carbon while keeping their stomata closed during the day—an obvious advantage for plants that must conserve water in the extremely dry conditions of a desert.

Chloroplast density in the bundle sheath cells of C_4 plants is much higher than in the surrounding mesophyll cells. A high chloroplast density is probably necessary to process the high carbon dioxide concentrations generated by the C_4 system. Finally, the cells which actually produce the sugar, the bundle sheath, are in direct contact with the vascular tissues responsible for exporting the sugar to other parts of the plant. The end result is that the C_4 arrangement contributes to higher productivity by overcoming the inefficiencies inherent in C_3 plants due to photorespiration. Under optimal conditions, the rate of carbon assimilation by C_4 crop plants can exceed that of C_3 crop plants by two or three times.

STARCH AND SUCROSE

We have seen that glyceraldehyde-3-phosphate (G3P) is the first sugar produced in the photosynthetic carbon reduction cycle. G3P is interchangeable with a close analog called **dihydroxyacetone phosphate (DHAP)**. Since both GAP and DHAP are three-carbon sugars, they are commonly referred to as **triose phosphates.** Where the triose phosphates go is determined largely by the demands of the plant for carbon and energy. They may be exported from the chloroplast to make sugars for other plant organs or they may be temporarily stored in the chloroplasts.

When carbon is needed elsewhere in the plant, the triose phosphates are transported across the chloroplast membrane to the cytoplasm of the surrounding cell, where they serve as building blocks for the synthesis of other sugars. One molecule each of G3P and DHAP first combine to form a molecule of the six-carbon glucose. Glucose is commonly referred to as grape sugar or fruit sugar because it is the principal sugar found in grapes and other sweet fruits. Glucose may also be referred to as dextrose. Glucose is interchangeable with fructose, another six-carbon sugar. When a molecule of glucose combines with a molecule of fructose, the product is the 12-carbon sugar

sucrose. Sucrose is important because not only because it is a major product of photosynthesis in green leaves, but it is also the principal form of sugar that is transported over long distances from leaves to stems and roots in most plants. Sucrose is the major storage carbon in plants such as sugar beet and sugarcane. Sucrose is common table sugar.

When photosynthesis is producing sugar faster than it can be exported from the leaf, it may be stored in the chloroplast as starch. In this case, the triose phosphate is retained in the chloroplast where is converted to glucose. The glucose molecules are then linked end-to-end to form long chains of **starch**. Starch is formed in the chloroplast stroma, where it accumulates as insoluble aggregates, or starch grains. In some situations, a starch grain may grow so large that it virtually takes over the entire chloroplast.

There is a very tight relationship between the metabolism of sucrose and starch that illustrates how the control of metabolism can be integrated between two compartments of the cell. During the middle of the day, when light intensity is highest, the supply of carbohydrate from the chloroplast may exceed the capacity of the cell to export sucrose. As sucrose accumulates in the cytosol, the flow of triose phosphate from the chloroplast is shut down. The increase of triose phosphate in the chloroplast in turn activates the enzymes necessary for conversion of triose phosphate to glucose and starch synthesis. As night approaches and the light intensity falls, the rate of photosynthesis progressively declines. The result is that decreasing amounts of triose phosphates are available for export to the cytosol and the rate of sucrose export will catch up with or exceed the rate of sucrose synthesis. Declining sucrose concentrations relieve the inhibition of triose phosphate export and the concentration of triose in the chloroplast will decline. Consequently, the breakdown of starch reserves will be favored over starch synthesis. The resulting breakdown products of starch are exported from the chloroplast to the cytosol, where they support continued sucrose synthesis and export from the leaf during the night.

Summary

Using several new experimental techniques, Melvin Calvin identified phosphoglyceric acid (PGA) as the first product of photosynthesis. He showed how carbon dioxide was incorporated into organic molecules and unraveled the mysteries of the photosynthetic carbon reduction (PCR) cycle.

The PCR cycle can be divided into three stages: the carboxylation stage, the reduction stage, and the regeneration stage. Energy in the form of ATP and NADPH, both products of the light reactions, is required for the reduction and regeneration stages, but not the fixation stage. The first sugar product of the PCR cycle is glyceraldehyde-3-phosphate, formed by reduction of PGA. Because carbon dioxide enters the cycle one molecule at a time and because some of the product must be used to regenerate the acceptor molecule, ribulose-1,5-bisphosphate, the cycle must turn six times to generate one six-carbon glucose molecule.

The carbon-fixing enzyme Rubisco also "fixes" oxygen, giving rise to the competing, light-dependent evolution of carbon dioxide referred to as photorespiration. Photorespiration is a costly process in terms of energy and carbon, losing as much as one-third of the carbon assimilated by photosynthesis. C_4 plants have evolved a modified pathway for fixing carbon that suppresses photorespiration and improves the overall efficiency of carbon fixation. C_4 photosynthesis is organized in two distinct cell types: mesophyll cells that contain the enzyme PEP carboxylase and bundle sheath cells that contain Rubisco. The PEP carboxylase initially "fixes" the carbon and pumps it into the bundle sheath cells, where the carbon is released and then enters the PCR cycle. By effectively increasing the ratio of carbon dioxide to oxygen in the bundle sheath, C_4 plants suppress photo-respiration. C_4 plants gain a particular advantage over C_3 plants under conditions of high light intensity and water stress.

Triose sugars formed by the PCR cycle are exported from the chloroplast into the cytoplasm of the leaf cell, where they are used to form sucrose. Sucrose is the principal form of sugar that is transported from the leaf cells to other cells and tissue in most plants. Alternatively, when the rate of photosynthesis exceeds the capacity to export sucrose, the triose sugars are retained in the chloroplast where they are stored in the form of starch.

5 Cellular Respiration
Retrieving Energy and Carbon

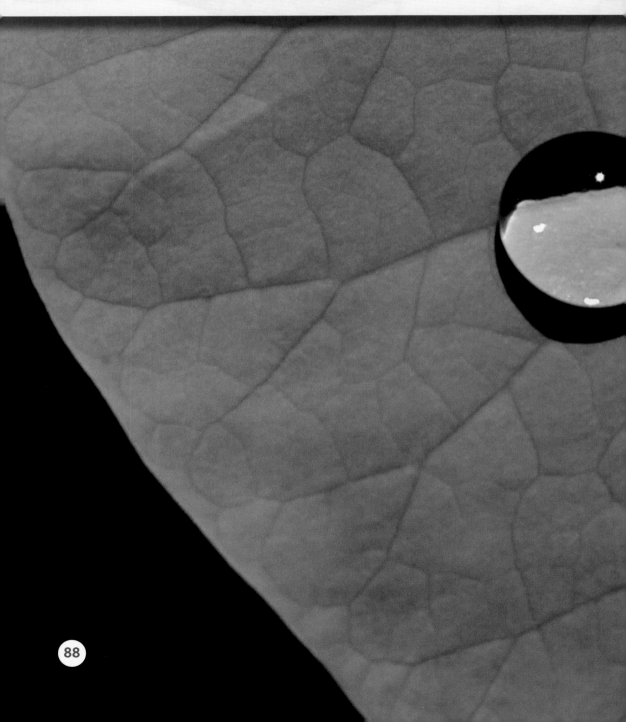

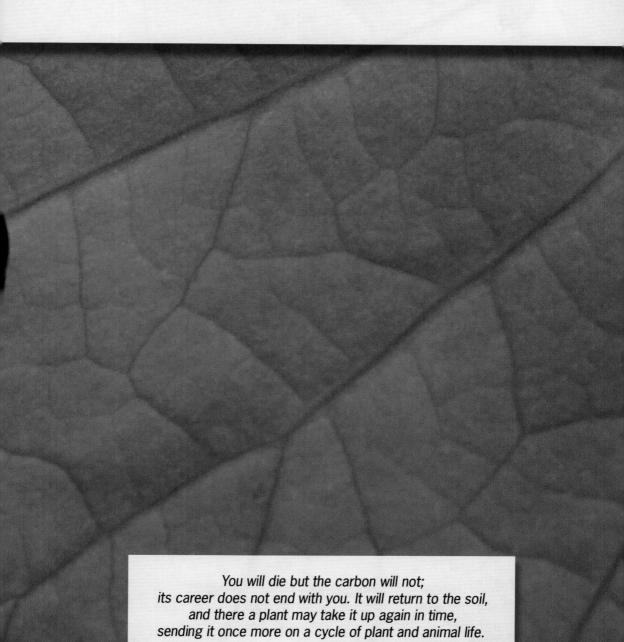

You will die but the carbon will not;
its career does not end with you. It will return to the soil,
and there a plant may take it up again in time,
sending it once more on a cycle of plant and animal life.

—Jacob Bronowski (1908—1974)
Mathematician, author

Cellular Respiration:
Retrieving Energy and Carbon

RETRIEVING THE ENERGY OF PHOTOSYNTHESIS

The energy-rich triose-phosphate molecules synthesized as a result of photosynthesis may be stored temporarily as starch in the chloroplast, but ultimately they will be exported to be used as a source of energy and carbon for synthetic activities and other forms of work elsewhere in the plant. This may include the leaf cells themselves or cells in the stems, roots, flowers, and other organs. These molecules may also be ingested by animals that eat the plants, again to be used as a source of energy and carbon for their activities.

As we learned earlier, these molecules are a source of free energy because they are chemically reduced. The energy stored in reduced molecules can be retrieved by removing electrons through chemical oxidation. The biochemical pathways that cells use to retrieve chemical energy are collectively called **cellular respiration.**

Although a variety of sugars, fats, and proteins can be broken down through respiration, we will focus on the oxidation of glucose by way of illustration. The complete oxidation of glucose is summarized in the following chemical equation:

$$C_6H_{12}O_6 + O_2 + 6H_2O \longrightarrow 6CO_2 + 12H_2O$$

For each mole (180 g) of glucose oxidized, 2,831 kJ of energy is released. Clearly, it would be of no benefit to a cell if this amount of energy were released all at once—the cell would literally burn up. Instead, cellular respiration oxidizes glucose and other energy sources in a series of small, enzyme-catalyzed steps. The result is a controlled release of energy in smaller packages that is far more useful. Most, but not all, of these reactions are carried out in a small cellular organelle called the **mitochondrion** (plural, mitochondria) and the energy released is used primarily and most immediately to synthesize ATP.

Respiration is divided into three distinct sequential pathways (Figure 5.1). In the initial pathway, called **glycolysis** (from the Greek *glycos* meaning "sugar" and *lysis* meaning "breaking apart"), glucose is converted to two molecules of pyruvic acid, or pyruvate. Pyruvic acid is the non-ionized form (–COOH) and pyruvate is the ionized form (–COO$^-$ + H$^+$); at pH values commonly found in cells, organic acids are normally present as the ionized form. Under **aerobic** conditions (when oxygen is available), pyruvate is further metabolized by the **citric acid cycle** and the **electron transport chain**. In the citric acid cycle, pyruvate is completely oxidized to carbon dioxide. Although a small amount of ATP is produced directly from both glycolysis and the citric acid cycle, most of the energy originally associated with glucose is conserved in the form of reduced electron carriers NADH and FADH$_2$. NADH and FADH$_2$ are then re-oxidized in the electron transport chain, which is also the principal ATP generator in the cell.

These core reactions that comprise cellular respiration are virtually identical in plants, animals, and microorganisms. You will also no doubt notice that many of the intermediates in respiration are substances used in photosynthetic carbon metabolism.

THE MITOCHONDRION

The enzymes that catalyze the reactions of glycolysis are located in the cytoplasm of the cell, but the citric acid cycle and the electron transport chain are located in the mitochondrion (Figure 5.2). Plant mitochondria are spherical or short rods that measure about 0.5 µm to 1.0 m in diameter by 1–3 m long. The number of mitochondria in a cell may vary from 200 to 2,000 per cell, depending on the level of metabolic activity. Cells with higher metabolic activity have greater energy demands and thus higher numbers of mitochondria.

Although the shape and size may vary, mitochondria from both plants and animals contain two membranes that divide the

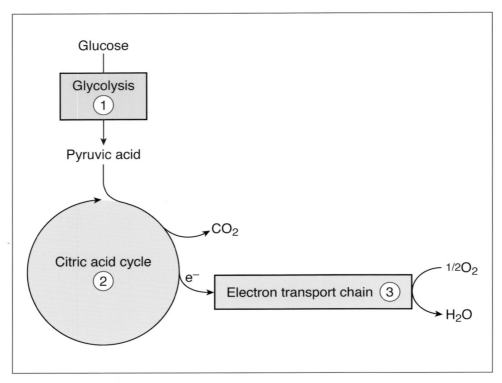

Figure 5.1 Cellular respiration is divided into three sequential pathways: (1) glycolysis, (2) the citric acid cycle, and (3) the electron transport chain.

organelle into four compartments: an outer membrane; an inner membrane; the space between the two membranes, called the intermembrane space; and the **matrix**, an unstructured aqueous region located within the inner membrane. The inner membrane has many inwardly directed folds, or invaginations, called **cristae** (singular, crista).

Each of the four compartments of the mitochondrion is the site of specific metabolic functions. The outer membrane, for example, separates the mitochondrion from the rest of the cytoplasm. It contains numerous pore-forming proteins that facilitate the movement of materials into and out of the mitochondrion. The inner membrane, including the cristae, is the

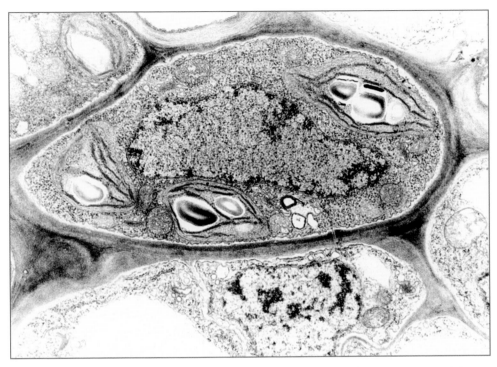

Figure 5.2 Like chloroplasts, mitochondria are limited by an outer and inner membrane. The mitochondrial inner membrane, however, is extensively infolded into a number of projections called cristae.

site of the electron transport chain and the matrix contains the enzymes of the citric acid cycle. The intermembrane space functions as a proton reservoir that is involved in ATP synthesis; the same function served by the lumen in the chloroplast (see Chapter 3).

GLYCOLYSIS

As with most endeavors, it is simply not possible to get a return without first making an investment. The same is true when attempting to retrieve energy from glucose. In fact, two molecules of ATP are consumed in the first three steps of glycolysis (Figure 5.3).

In the first step, one ATP is used to convert glucose to glucose-1-phosphate. Then, in two steps, glucose-1-phosphate is converted to fructose-6-phosphate and another ATP is used to form fructose-1,6-bisphosphate. These steps are necessary because glucose is a relatively stable molecule—it is not readily broken down and must be activated before any energy can be retrieved. The two phosphorylations are analogous to priming a pump and the two ATP will returned with interest later in glycolysis.

In preparation for the energy-conserving reactions to come, fructose-1,6-bisphosphate is split into two molecules of glyceraldehyde-3-phosphate (GAP). Note that since the original

Chloroplasts and Mitochondria

When viewed in the electron microscope, chloroplasts and mitochondria look different, but they are structurally and functionally similar. Both are energy transducing organelles—they convert energy from one form to another. Both are limited by an inner and an outer membrane, have a system of inner membranes that contain redox carriers and an unstructured matrix that contains enzymes for carbon metabolism, and both use the same chemiosmotic mechanism that links the free energy of electron transport to the synthesis of ATP.

Structurally, chloroplasts differ from mitochondria in that the internal membranes, the energy-transducing thylakoids, are separate from the inner limiting membrane, while the equivalent membranes in mitochondria, the cristae, are continuous with the inner membrane. But if you can imagine a crista pinching off where it joins the inner membrane, it would form a closed vesicle that is equivalent to a chloroplast thylakoid. In that case, the lumen of the thylakoid would be structurally and functionally equivalent to the inner membrane space in the mitochondrion. This is another example of common principles that are fundamental to seemingly diverse organs and organisms throughout the realm of biology.

six-carbon glucose molecule has now been split into two three-carbon molecules, it is necessary from this point on to multiply everything by two in order to account for the original glucose molecule. In the next step, called oxidative phosphorylation, GAP is oxidized to form 1,3-bisphosphoglyceric acid (BPG). In this reaction, the energy of oxidation is conserved in two forms: to reduce NAD^+ to NADH and also to add a second phosphate group to GAP without involving ATP.

In the final steps of glycolysis, the two phosphate groups are transferred from 1,3-bisphosphate to ADP, thus conserving energy as ATP. With the completion of glycolysis, there has been

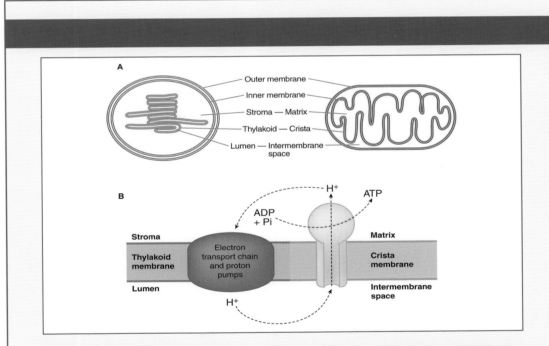

Although chloroplasts and mitochondria may look quite different, they are actually very similar. (A) The equivalence of the five metabolic compartments in the two organelles is shown. (B) Both organelles use electron transport to establish a proton gradient that fuels ATP synthesis.

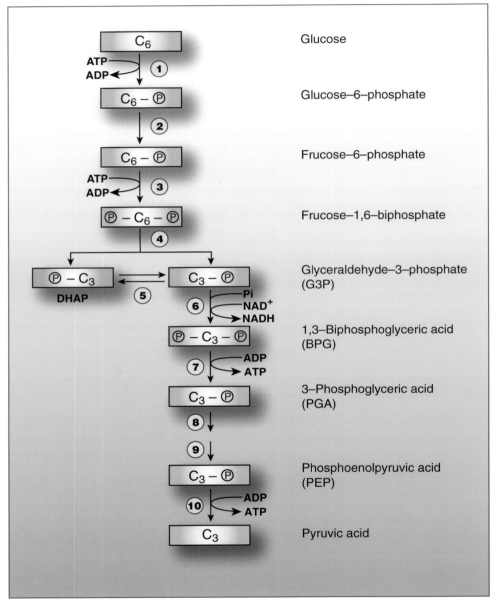

Figure 5.3 The reactions of glycolysis take place in the cell cytoplasm. A specific enzyme is involved at each step in the pathway. The overall result of glycolysis is to convert one molecule of glucose (C_6) into two molecules of pyruvic acid (C_3). There is no loss of carbon dioxide and a minimal yield of ATP.

no loss of carbon—all six carbon atoms of the original glucose molecule are accounted for in the two molecules of the final product, pyruvate. The energy of two ATP molecules was invested in the beginning but four ATP were produced for a net gain of two ATP. Additional energy was conserved in the form of two molecules of NADH (Figure 5.4).

The fate of pyruvate depends on whether or not oxygen is present (Figure 5.5). For organisms that are able to survive in the absence of oxygen, such as **anaerobic** microorganisms, this is as far as it goes. Some microorganisms, such as yeast, will further metabolize pyruvate to ethanol and human muscle tissue will form lactic acid (the cause of sore muscles) when in oxygen debt. Metabolism of pyruvate under anaerobic conditions is known as **fermentation.**

In the presence of oxygen, pyruvate is transported into the mitochondrion, where it enters the citric acid cycle and electron transport system and is completely oxidized to carbon dioxide and water. Higher plants are **obligate aerobes**, meaning that they can only briefly survive in the absence of oxygen. Even higher plants, however, can experience temporary anaerobiosis, such as in roots when the soil is saturated with water. In root cells, the primary fermentation products are carbon dioxide and water. Roots can undergo fermentation only briefly before the cells begin to die.

THE CITRIC ACID CYCLE

The citric acid cycle is known by several names, including the tri-carboxylic acid (TCA) cycle and the Krebs cycle (after its discoverer, Hans Krebs). The citric acid cycle leads to the stepwise oxidation of pyruvate to carbon dioxide. As pyruvate is progressively oxidized, electrons are transferred to NAD and FAD and one molecule of ATP is synthesized directly from ADP and P_i. All of these reactions occur within the matrix of the mitochondrion.

The first loss of carbon as carbon dioxide comes as pyruvate is prepared for entry into the citric acid cycle. Remember that

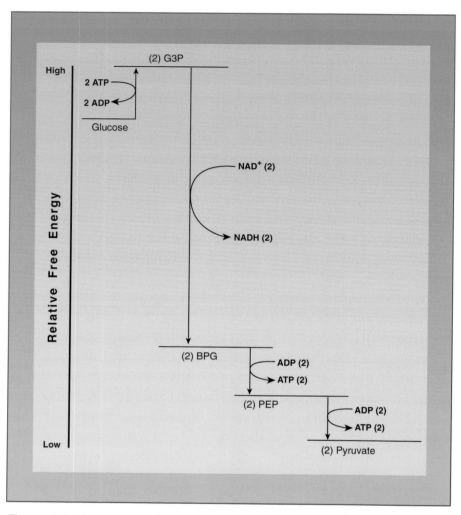

Figure 5.4 Free energy changes in glycolysis as glucose is broken down to pyruvate. After investing two ATP to activate glucose, the major energy drop is between glyceraldehyde-3-phosphate (G3P) and 1, 3-bisphosphoglycerate (BPG). Smaller drops occur in the conversion of BPG to phosphoenolpyruvate (PEP) and to pyruvate. In these two steps, more ATP is conserved.

pyruvate was formed in the cytosol, so in order to be oxidized by the citric acid cycle, pyruvate must be transported across the two mitochondrial membranes to the mitochondrial

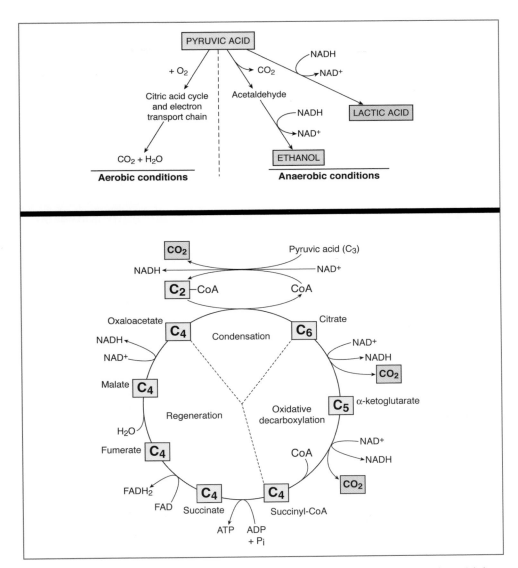

Figure 5.5 (A) The fate of pyruvic acid is determined by the presence (aerobic) or absence (anaerobic) of oxygen. In the presence of oxygen, pyruvate is transferred into the mitochondrion, where it is further oxidized to carbon dioxide and water. In the absence of oxygen, mitochondrial respiration will shut down and metabolism shifts to fermentation. (B) The citric acid cycle completes the oxidation of pyruvate to carbon dioxide. A small amount of ATP is formed by substrate level phosphory-lation, but most of the energy is conserved in the form of reduced redox carriers NADH and $FADH_2$.

matrix. Here, it becomes the substrate for a multi-enzyme complex called **pyruvate dehydrogenase**. This complex contains three enzymes catalyzing at least three different reactions. The

Enzymes and Vitamins

Although enzymes catalyze a wide variety of chemical reactions, there are certain reactions, such as oxidation-reduction and group transfer reactions that require the participation of smaller molecules called cofactors or **coenzymes** in association with the enzyme. NAD and NADP are examples of coenzymes that participate in oxidation-reduction reactions. Coenzyme A is an example of a coenzyme involved in group transfer reactions. Most animals, including humans, are not able to synthesize critical portions of coenzymes, so these precursors must be present in their diet. These are the molecules known as vitamins. The only exception to the rule is calciferol, or vitamin D, which can be synthesized by the human body.

Many vitamins required in the human diet are cofactors for respiratory enzymes. The nicotinamide portion of NAD and NADP and its carboxylic acid precursor nicotinic acid, for example, are listed on your breakfast cereal box as nicotinamide (or niacinamide) and niacin, respectively. The pyruvate dehydrogenase complex requires thiamine pyrophosphate (vitamin B_1) as a coenzyme. Riboflavin (vitamin B_2) is a component of flavinadenine dinucleotide or FAD and the vitamin pantothenic acid is a component of coenzyme A.

These are just some examples of the vitamins you need to keep your energy metabolism functioning properly. Does this mean that you can increase your energy by taking vitamin supplements? Not necessarily, especially if you are a healthy adult who eats a balanced diet. Not surprisingly, plants are able to synthesize these molecules on their own, so a diet that includes whole grains, fruits, and fresh green vegetables will provide most of the vitamins you need. Vitamins are just another good reason to eat your veggies!

overall result of these reactions is that pyruvate is oxidized and one molecule of NAD^+ is reduced to NADH. At the same time, pyruvate loses a molecule of carbon dioxide, leaving a two-carbon acetyl group. The acetyl group is not free but is combined with a small molecule called coenzyme A before it is released from pyruvate dehydrogenase. This complex is called acetyl coenzyme A, or acetyl CoA. Incidentally, acetyl CoA is the principal breakdown product from the fatty acid component of fats and oils, so when fatty acids are metabolized for energy, they enter respiration at this point.

The citric acid cycle can also be thought of as occurring in three stages: a condensation reaction, oxidative decarboxylation, and regeneration (see Figure 5.5). The first step in the citric acid cycle is called a condensation reaction because acetyl CoA donates its two-carbon acetyl group to a C_4 organic acid oxaloacetate (OAA), thus forming citric acid or citrate, a C_6 tricarboxylic acid.

In the oxidative decarboxylation stage, citrate is successively oxidized to alpha-ketoglutarate (C_5) and succinate (C_4). At each step, a molecule of NAD is reduced to NADH and a molecule of carbon dioxide is given off. These two oxidative decarboxylations effectively complete the breakdown of pyruvate. In addition, one molecule of ATP is formed from ADP and P_i. This ATP formation is called a substrate-level phosphorylation to contrast it with the oxygen-dependent phosphorylation we will talk about as part of the electron transport chain.

The conversion of succinate to fumarate is another oxidation that initiates the regeneration stage. Both succinate and fumerate are C_4 acids, but a carbon-carbon single bond in succinate has been converted to a carbon-carbon double bond in fumerate, with the loss of two electrons and two protons. These electrons and protons are transferred to FAD, reducing it to $FADH_2$. Next, a molecule of water is added to the double bond in fumerate. This restores the single bond and adds a hydroxyl group to form malate. Oxidation of malate brings us back to oxaloacetate, which is where we started. The oxaloacetate is ready to pick up another acetyl group and start the cycle all over again.

With each turn of the citric acid cycle, one molecule of pyruvate is completely oxidized to three molecules of carbon dioxide. In addition, four molecules of NADH, one molecule of $FADH_2$, and one molecule of ATP have been generated. Remember, though, that each pyruvate that goes through the cycle represents only half of a glucose molecule, so to account for the glucose that we started with, these numbers must be multiplied by two. To this we must also add the two ATP and two NADH gained in the course of glycolysis for a total of four ATP, 10 NADH, and two $FADH_2$.

THE MITOCHONDRIAL ELECTRON TRANSPORT CHAIN

At this point, the glucose has been completely oxidized to carbon dioxide, but we still haven't generated much ATP. In addition, this is supposed to be about aerobic (oxygen-dependent) respiration, but no oxygen has yet been involved. On the other hand, there are a number of electron pairs that have been removed from citric acid cycle intermediates and used to form the energy-rich molecules NADH and $FADH_2$.

THow much free energy is conserved in those electron pairs? We can estimate that value by multiplying the number of reduced electron carriers generated in both glycolysis and the citric acid cycle multiplied by the value of the free energy that would be released if they were transferred to oxygen.

Free energy kJ/mole	#	Total free energy
NADH	221 x 10	= 2210
$FADH_2$	180 x 2	= 360
		Total 2,570

If we then divide this total by the free energy of oxidation of glucose, which is 2,831 kJ/mol, 91% of the energy of the glucose molecule has been conserved in reduced electron carriers. If we also take into account the four ATP (at 31 kJ/mol each) that were generated in glycolysis and the citric acid cycle, the calculated efficiency of energy conservation at this stage rises to 95%.

We calculated the energy of NADH and $FADH_2$ by assuming their electrons were transferred to molecular oxygen because that is exactly what happens in the third phase of respiration, the electron transport chain. Both NADH and $FADH_2$ can be oxidized by molecular oxygen as shown in the following equations:

$$2NADH + 2H^+ + O_2 \longrightarrow 2NAD^+ + 2H_2O$$

$$2FADH_2 + O_2 \longrightarrow 2FAD + 2H_2O$$

As was the case with the breakdown of glucose, these oxidations are not accomplished in a single step. Instead, the electrons are passed through a series of electron carriers, each of which is alternately reduced and re-oxidized, until the electrons are finally passed to oxygen (Figure 5.6). This sequence of carriers is known as the electron transport chain and oxygen is the terminal electron acceptor in the chain. The principal components of the electron transport chain are all located in the inner mitochondrial membrane or cristae.

As the name implies, the electron transport chain carries electrons but not protons. This can be explained by the fact that the principal electron carriers in the chain are cytochromes, the same kinds of molecules that carry electrons between PSII and PSI in photosynthesis (see Chapter 3). Remember that cytochromes carry only electrons, so the protons given up when NADH and $FADH_2$ are initially oxidized are simply released into the proton pool in the mitochondrial matrix. When oxygen is finally reduced at the end of the chain, the protons required to form water are simply drawn from that same aqueous pool.

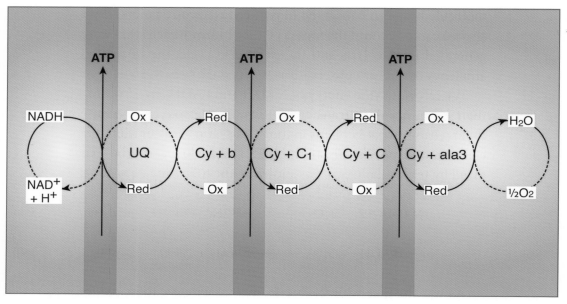

Figure 5.6 The electron transport chain is like a "bucket brigade"—electrons are passed from one cytochrome molecule to the next until they are finally passed to oxygen, which is reduced to water. Experiments using inhibitors that block electron flow at different locations have indicated three locations where ATP is formed. Because ATP formation in this case is oxygen-dependent, it is called oxidative phosphorylation.

As the electrons are passed between carriers in the electron transport chain, there is a stepwise drop in energy and the free energy released is used to generate ATP. When electrons are donated to the chain from NADH, three molecules of ATP are generated and when they are donated from $FADH_2$, two molecules of ATP are generated. The formation of ATP as electrons are passed to molecular oxygen is commonly known as **oxidative phosphorylation**.

ATP SYNTHESIS AND ELECTRON TRANSPORT

ATP synthesis is coupled to electron transport in the mitochondrion by the same chemiosmotic mechanism that is used in the chloroplast (see Chapter 3). Like the photosynthetic electron transport chain, the mitochondrial electron transport chain is composed of several multiprotein complexes. In the mitochondrion, there are four such complexes, each containing the enzymes and cofactors necessary to carry out only a portion of the electron transport chain (Figure 5.7). In addition, there are two smaller molecules—ubiquinone (UQ) and **cytochrome c**—that diffuse freely within the membrane and convey electrons between the four large complexes.

Experiments employing inhibitors that were able to block electron transport at specific locations led to the identification of three sites in the electron transport chain where sufficient free energy is made available to drive ATP synthesis. Each of the three phosphorylation sites corresponds to one of the electron transport complexes. As might be expected then, these three membrane complexes also function as proton pumps; some of the energy of electron transport is used to establish a proton gradient across the inner membrane. In this case, the protons are pumped from the matrix into the intermembrane space between the inner and outer mitochondrial membrane. Again, like the chloroplast thylakoid membrane, the inner mitochondrial membrane also contains an ATP synthetase enzyme that uses the energy of the proton gradient to synthesize ATP.

Several poisons, including azide, and hydrogen cyanide (HCN, or prussic acid), are highly toxic to organisms that depend on aerobic respiration because they interfere with mitochondrial electron transport. Azide and cyanide irreversibly bind to the cytochrome a/a_3 complex (also known as cytochrome oxidase) and block the final transfer of electrons to oxygen. As a result, the electron transport chain shuts down, protons are no longer pumped across the membrane, and the cell can no longer make ATP. Without ATP, virtually none of the cells vital functions are possible and cell death quickly follows.

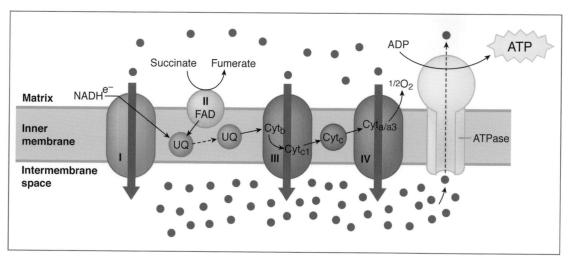

Figure 5.7 The mitochondrial electron transport chain is organized into four multi-protein complexes. Three of the complexes (I, III, IV) span the membrane and serve to pump protons and transport electrons. The fourth complex contains FAD and accepts electrons directly from succinate. Two other components, ubiquinone (UQ) and cytochrome c (cytc) are mobile carriers that diffuse in the membrane and transfer electrons between the major complexes. FAD donates its electron directly to ubiquinone. Like the thylakoid membrane, the mitochondrial membrane also includes the enzyme ATP synthetase (ATPase).

Other poisons that inhibit oxidative electron transport at other locations in the chain include rotenone (a plant toxin), amytal (a barbiturate), and antimycin A (an antibiotic). Rotenone is found in the roots, bark, and seeds of *Lonchocarpus* and several other tropical plants that are used as a fish poison by natives in eastern Africa and South America. Rotenone decomposes rapidly when exposed to light and air, so natives are able to eat harvested fish without ill effect. Because rotenone is a natural toxin and is short-lived in the environment, it is also used as an insecticide in organic gardening.

CARBON BUILDING BLOCKS

The significance of respiration to a cell is not limited to the generation of ATP and reducing potential. While energy is certainly needed to build the stuff of which cells are made, carbon is also needed. The intermediates in glycolysis and citric acid cycle are the carbon building blocks for cellulose, proteins, fatty acids, nucleic acids, pigments, hormones, and all the other molecules that make up a cell. Another principal function of cellular respiration is to modify the carbon skeletons of storage

How Cells Regulate Glucose Metabolism

Respiration is most efficient when sufficient glucose is oxidized to meet only the cell's immediate metabolic demands. One of the ways cells balance glucose oxidation against metabolic demand is to monitor ATP turnover and, through a type of feedback control, adjust the activity of glycolytic and citric acid cycle enzymes. This works in part because electron transport through the electron transport chain and ATP synthesis are tightly coupled to proton pumping.

When cells are metabolically active and the demand for energy is high, ATP turns over very quickly. The increased availability of ADP and inorganic phosphate stimulates ATPase to make more ATP. As the rate of ATP synthesis increases, the proton gradient dissipates more rapidly, which, in turn, accelerates the rate of NADH oxidation by the electron transport chain. Several critical enzymes in glycolysis and the citric acid cycle are sensitive to the ratio of NADH to NAD. Rising levels of NAD stimulate the activities of these enzymes and glucose is metabolized more quickly.

On the other hand, when the rate of ATP utilization decreases due to a drop in metabolic demand the return of protons through ATPase will slow down and the proton gradient will increase. The gradient may increase to the point where the electron transport chain can no longer supply the amount of energy that is required to pump additional protons across the membrane. The oxidation of NADH then slows down, increasing the NADH/NAD ratio, and the enzymes of glycolysis and the citric acid cycle will respond by slowing down glucose oxidation.

compounds such as sucrose and starch to form these essential building blocks.

A few examples should suffice to indicate the importance of this role for respiration. We mentioned earlier that the breakdown of **fatty acids** yielded two-carbon acetate fragments and acetyl CoA was the point of entry for fatty acids into respiration. The reverse is also true: fatty acids are synthesized by linking together acetate fragments carried by acetyl CoA. Acetyl CoA is also the starting point for the synthesis of carotenoids, the phytol tail of chlorophyll, and gibberellins (a class of plant hormones). Phosphoenolpyruvate, pyruvate, oxaloacetate, and alpha-keotglutarate are all precursors to the 20 amino acids that make up proteins. Glucose phosphate is linked together to make the cellulose of plant cell walls or it may be converted to the ribose and deoxyribose found in ATP and NAD(H).

Summary

Respiration is a process that retrieves light energy that was stored in the chemical bonds of a glucose molecule and converts this energy to ATP, a universal mobile energy carrier. The key to understanding respiration is to follow the electrons and protons.

As glucose is oxidized to carbon dioxide through glycolysis and the citric acid cycle, the free energy of oxidation is conserved by transferring electrons to the coenzymes NAD^+ and FAD. The reduced coenzymes are then re-oxidized by donating their electrons to oxygen via the electron transport chain. The free energy released in three different steps in the chain is stored temporarily by pumping protons across the inner mitochondrial membrane.

The proton gradient collapses by channeling protons through the membrane-bound enzyme ATPase, which uses the free energy stored in the proton gradient to synthesize ATP. The ATP is then transported out of the mitochondrion to other regions of the cell to perform various kinds of work for the cell. Cellular respiration also converts simple sugars into the carbon building blocks that are used for the synthesis of more complex molecules.

Photosynthesis and the Environment

*Like a great poet,
Nature knows how to produce
the greatest effects with the most limited means.*

— Heinrich Heine (1797—1856)
German poet, critic

Photosynthesis and the Environment

CARBON ASSIMILATION

The previous chapters have focused on the biochemical aspects of photosynthesis and respiration at the subcellular, cellular, and tissue or organ level. The balance between photosynthesis and respiration determines the amount of carbon assimilation by a plant, which extends well beyond the performance of individual plants. Carbon assimilation by plants creates biomass, or organic matter, that supports humans and virtually all other heterotrophs in the biosphere. Since the beginning of the Industrial Revolution, a burgeoning human population has put increasing pressure on the biosphere for food, building materials, and urban development. These pressures have in turn generated interest in factors that increase biomass, or productivity.

Understanding productivity has obvious relevance to agriculture, but it also has implications for ecological research because it helps to understand problems of nutrient and energy flow through communities. Productivity has implications for the upper limits of the Earth's capacity to sustain human populations and our ability to manage world resources.

There are a variety of environmental factors, such as light, availability of carbon dioxide, soil, water, and nutrients that can influence photosynthesis and productivity. A complete discussion of the factors that influence photosynthesis and plant productivity is beyond the scope of this book, but we will discuss a few of the more important factors in order to illustrate the kinds of problems and solutions involved.

LIMITS ON PHOTOSYNTHESIS

When the stomata are open, there is a constant exchange of carbon dioxide between a leaf and the surrounding atmosphere. The actual amount of CO_2 taken up is the balance between CO_2 uptake for photosynthesis and CO_2 evolution from photorespiration and cellular respiration. This balance is called the net **carbon exchange rate** (**CER**). In the dark or in light levels barely

112

sufficient to drive photosynthesis, the CER is actually negative (Figure 6.1). This means that the rate of CO_2 evolution from respiration is greater than the rate of uptake for photosynthesis. As light levels increase, respiration remains constant but photosynthesis and, consequently, CO_2 uptake increases. The point where CER reaches zero is called the **light compensation point**. At this point, the light level is high enough that CO_2 uptake for photosynthesis "compensates" for the CO_2 evolved by respiration.

For most plants, the light compensation point is equivalent to a well-lighted office or classroom. With increasing light beyond the compensation point, the CER continues to increase until a light saturation level is reached and further increases in light result in little or no increase in CER. A C_3 plant typically reaches light saturation at one-quarter to one-half of full sunlight. At light saturation, photosynthesis in no longer limited by light—it is now limited by the concentration of CO_2 in the air. Beyond the point of light saturation, further increases in the rate of photosynthesis can be achieved only by increasing the amount of CO_2 in the atmosphere. It appears that CO_2 is often the limiting factor in photosynthesis, at least in C_3 plants.

Unlike C_3 plants, C_4 plants never really reach light saturation (see Figure 6.1). This is probably due to the absence of photorespiration and the fact that C_4 plants are able to continue to fix carbon even when the stomata are partially closed and CO_2 concentrations inside the leaf are low (see Chapter 4). C_4 plants are able to use this extra light energy to drive the phosphoenolpyruvate-based carbon dioxide pump, which may account, in part, for the high productivity of C_4 crops such as sugarcane and corn. Did you know that when the sun is bright, temperatures are high, and there is plenty of moisture in the ground, a field of corn will grow so fast that you can actually hear it grow?

Carbon dioxide–limited photosynthesis is a practical problem for commercial greenhouses, especially those engaged in the

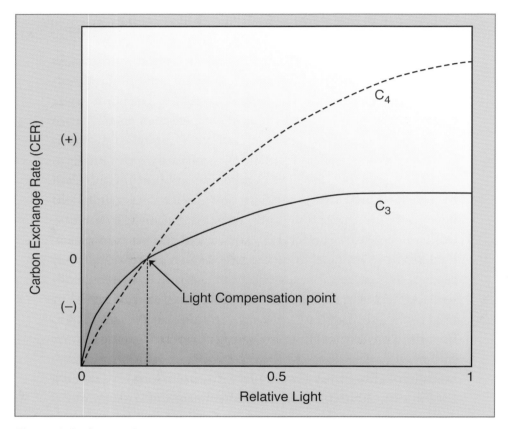

Figure 6.1 C_3 and C_4 plants respond to increasing light. A light level of 1 equals full sunlight. The carbon exchange rate (CER) is the difference between CO_2 uptake by photosynthesis and CO_2 evolution by photorespiration and mitochondrial respiration. The light level at which the two are balanced (CER = 0) is called the light compensation point. C_3 plants are light saturated above half of full sunlight, but C_4 plants never achieve light saturation.

production of flowers such as carnations, orchids, and roses, or vegetable crops such as lettuce, tomatoes, and cucumbers. This is especially true in winter when greenhouse ventilation is reduced in order to conserve heat and access to CO_2 from outside is restricted. Flower and vegetable crops will grow significantly faster and increase yields when the atmosphere is enriched with carbon dioxide during daylight hours, a practice known as CO_2 fertilization. In practice, the CO_2 content may be increased by 150–200 ppm to a total of perhaps 1.5 times atmospheric levels, although some foliage plant growers may supplement with CO_2 up to a total of 700–1,000 ppm.

LEAF AND CANOPY STRUCTURE INFLUENCE LIGHT

Within a population of plants (a forest or corn field, for example), the amount of light received by any given leaf is influenced by its position within the canopy. Leaves at the outer surface of the canopy receive direct light on their upper surfaces and diffuse, or scattered, light on their lower surfaces. Leaves lower down in the canopy receive progressively less direct light and must depend on the occasional sun fleck—a spot of direct sunlight—or diffuse light. The composition of light also changes as it moves downward through the canopy. The outer leaves, of course, filter out much of the photosynthetically active radiation (PAR), leaving the light available to lower leaves rich in the far-red and green but poor in the blue and red portions of the spectrum.

Often, the light reaching older, more mature leaves in the bottom of a canopy may fall below the light compensation point during a large part of the day. Curiously, perhaps because they are mature leaves that are no longer actively growing, respiration is also reduced along with reduced photosynthesis. So, while these interior leaves no longer contribute to net photosynthesis, neither do they become a drain on carbon resources through excessive respiration. Most plants avoid the cost of maintaining such nonproductive leaves by a process known as sequential **senescence**: older leaves lower down in the canopy senesce and die off as new leaves are formed at the top of the canopy. This is why the understory of mature forests is usually very open, with leaves only at the very top of the trees.

In agricultural settings, it is often important to maximize utilization of the incidental light. As a farmer, your job is to produce a maximum amount of harvestable biomass on a given plot of land. Since light that falls on bare ground makes no contribution to productivity, you would plant the seed close together. This ensures that the young plants cover the ground rapidly in order to maximize interception of light and, consequently, plant growth. On the other hand, too high a planting density means that the leaves will eventually overlap and shade each other as the plants grow larger and the canopy expands.

Farmers know, mostly through trial and error, what planting density gives the best yield for their crop, but there is a quantitative measure that helps optimize light interception and biomass in crop species—**leaf area index (LAI)**. LAI is a ratio of the leaf area (one surface only) of the crop to the ground area. The general relationship between LAI and biomass production is shown in Figure 6.2. The value for optimum LAI varies, but in productive agricultural ecosystems it typically falls in the range of 3 to 5. This means that for optimal light interception, there should be 3–5 square meters of leaf surface for each square meter of soil surface. The optimum LAI actually depends on the angle of the leaf to the stem. Horizontal leaves in dicotyledonous crops such as beans or clover absorb light efficiently, but also tend to overlap and therefore shade leaves lower in the canopy. Crops with horizontal leaves perform better at less than 3 LAIs. Erect leaves, typical of grass crops like rice, wheat, and corn, are less efficient at intercepting light, but can be planted at higher densities (and higher LAIs) because the leaves produce less shading. Depending on the angle of the leaves, grass crops may perform well with LAIs up to 7 or 8.

Corn breeders have attempted to breed plants with more erect leaves that would allow higher plant densities, but, in fact, the ideal corn plant has vertical upper leaves and more horizontal lower leaves. This pattern allows for a more uniform distribution of light through the canopy and, consequently, more efficient photosynthesis. It appears, however, that nature figured this

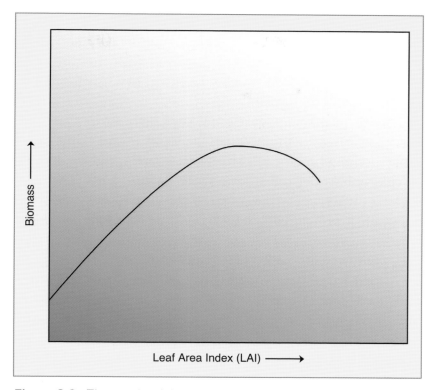

Biomass

Leaf Area Index (LAI) ⟶

Figure 6.2 The productivity, or increase in biomass, of a stand of plants increases as the leaf area index increases—up to the point where mutual shading of the leaves decreases light absorption and photosynthesis. Farmers will adjust planting density of their crops to achieve an optimum leaf area index and maximum biomass production.

out first, because most plants seem to have evolved with leaves spaced vertically on the stem at a distance at least twice their width. This pattern seems to allow an optimal balance between direct and diffuse light.

ADAPTING TO LIFE IN THE SHADE

The two photosystems with their built-in antennas serve well for plants growing in full sunlight, but not all plants grow in sunlight with a plentiful supply of photons. Many grow in varying degrees of shade under canopies where the light levels may be half or even one-tenth of full sunlight and the light harvesting capacity of the two photosystems, even with their antenna chlorophyll, will not provide enough energy to satisfy the photo-synthetic needs of the plant.

Shaded plants compensate for lower light levels in several ways: the leaves are thinner than the leaves of sun plants of the same species, with generally larger surface areas, and the number of chloroplasts per cell is lower·than in sun plants. The most striking difference, however, is the presence of two additional chlorophyll-protein complexes called **light-harvesting complexes.** There are two light-harvesting complexes—one associated with each photosystem—called LHCII and LHCI.

A light-harvesting complex may be thought of as a super antenna system that facilitates harvesting of available photons and thus helps to maintain a reasonable rate of photosynthesis under low light conditions. The light-harvesting complex is not a permanent part of the photosystem, but will attach to the core antenna of the photosystem when additional light-harvesting capacity is required (Figure 6.3). The significance of the light-harvesting complexes is perhaps indicated by the fact that together LHCI and LHCII may contain as much as 70% of the total chloroplast pigment in a shade plant.

Light-harvesting complexes are also present in plants grow-ing in moderate to high light intensities, although in somewhat lower quantities. Consider, for example, a plant growing in an exposed environment where it is subject to bright sun under cloudless skies. Under these conditions, this plant does not require an augmented antenna, so any LHCII present will detach from PSII in order to reduce the photon load on the reaction center. When heavy cloud cover moves in, however, the light level can drop significantly and, when it does, LHCII will once again attach to PSII. By being somewhat mobile, the light-harvesting complex allows for a dynamic adjustment

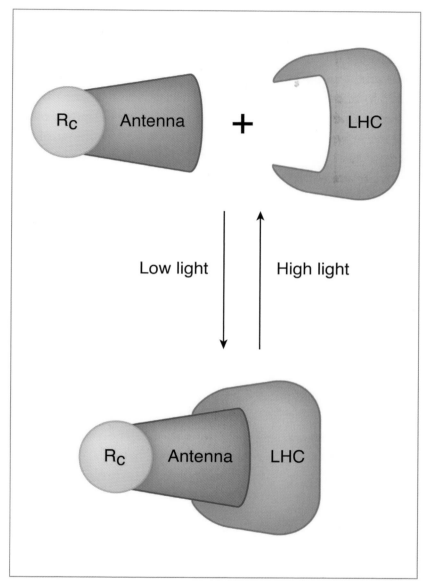

Figure 6.3 Plants adapt to shade or low-light conditions by synthesizing additional light-harvesting complexes (LHC). By attaching to the photosystem, the LHC increases the size of the antenna and the capacity of the photosystem to capture photons. Under high-light conditions, the LHC will detach to avoid excessive excitation and damage to the reaction center (Rc).

of photon energy input under conditions of fluctuating light intensity.

Plants also adjust to changing light levels by reorienting the chloroplasts in the palisade mesophyll cells. Chloroplasts do not have a fixed position but are constantly on the move with the rest of the protoplasm as it streams around the outer periphery of the cell, a phenomenon known as protoplasmic streaming. However, in very intense light, the disk-shaped chloroplasts tend to gather along the lateral cell walls to minimize photon capture by presenting their thin edge to the incoming light (Figure 6.4). On the other hand, the chloroplasts tend to maximize photon capture in low light levels by gathering along the upper and lower walls, thus presenting their broad surfaces to the light.

Plants growing in full sun face another potential problem—too much light can actually be harmful. During periods of peak light intensity, even rapidly growing crop plants may be able to use no more than 50% of the absorbed radiation. If the excess energy is not dissipated, it can actually damage the PSII reaction center and lead to a decrease in photosynthesis. This effect is called **photoinhibition**. Protection against photoinhibition is thought to be a primary function of the carotenoid pigments such as beta-carotene. The carotenoids intercept excess excitation energy from the antenna chlorophyll before it reaches the reaction center. The carotenoids then dissipate the energy harmlessly as heat.

TEMPERATURE, MOISTURE, AND PLANT DISTRIBUTION

Temperature is an obvious environmental factor that limits the distribution of plants. Many plants will grow only in the warm tropics, others find temperate regions more to their liking, while still others are limited to the colder, more northerly regions. In all cases, the plant growth can be described in terms of three cardinal temperatures (Figure 6.5). The temperatures at which biological processes can occur is general limited by the freezing

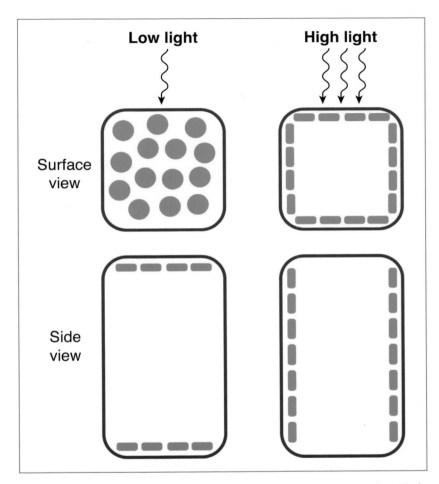

Figure 6.4 Chloroplasts adjust to light conditions by altering their position in the cell. Under low-light conditions, the discoid-shaped plastids accumulate at the upper and lower cell surfaces. In this orientation, their broad surfaces are presented to the light to maximize photon collection. Under high-light conditions, the plastids will accumulate along the lateral cell walls. In this orientation, the plastid's narrow edges are presented to the light to minimize photon collection.

point of water on the low side and irreversible denaturation of proteins on the high side.

Although the temperature response curve for growth represents the sum of temperature response curves for all enzyme

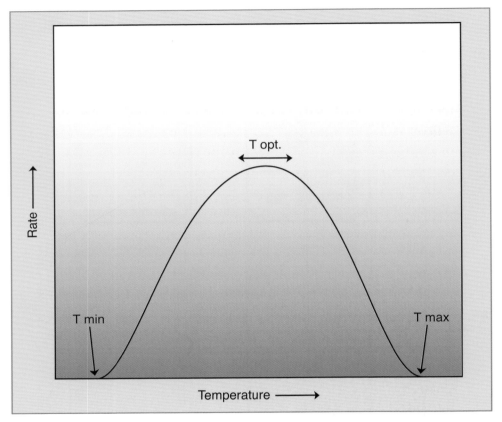

Figure 6.5 The response of every biological reaction to temperature can be described in terms of three cardinal temperatures: the lowest (Tmin) and highest (Tmax) temperatures at which the reaction will proceed and the optimum temperature (Topt) that allows for the maximum rate of the reaction. The cardinal temperatures for photosynthesis are determined by the temperature characteristics of critical enzymes.

reactions in the plant, the growth response curve typically reflects the temperature response curve for photosynthesis more than any other individual process. C_3 plants, for example, typically have an optimum temperature for both growth and photosynthesis in the range of 25°C to 30°C, while the optimum for growth and photosynthesis in C_4 plants may be in the range of 40°C to 50°C.

The presence of photorespiration in C_3 plants and its virtual absence from C_4 plants is a key factor in the sensitivity of these two kinds of plants to temperature and, consequently, in their distribution. For a variety of reasons, higher temperatures favor photorespiration over photosynthesis. In particular, at higher temperatures oxygenation of Rubisco is favored over carboxylation and some enzymes of the C_4 cycle are more stable than those of the C_3 cycle. The result is that the optimum temperature for photosynthesis in C_3 species is approximately 25°C (77°F), while C_4 species continue to photosynthesize at 30°C to 45°C (86°F to 113°F).

Worldwide, response to temperature and moisture are probably the most important factors affecting the distribution of C_3 and C_4 plants. Several studies of the distribution of grasses on mountain slopes in Hawaii, Africa, and Costa Rica have shown that C_4 grasses are predominant on the warmer, drier lower slopes of mountains, while the cooler, moist environments higher up the mountains tend to be populated primarily by C_3 grasses. The transition point between the two populations is the altitude at which the maximum daily temperature for the warmest month of the year is approximately 20°C (68°F).

Other studies have shown that similar principles apply to the latitudinal (north-south) distribution of C_4 and C_3 plants in North America. C_4 species tend to be found in more southerly or semitropical habitats, while the more northerly latitudes are inhabited almost exclusively by C_3 species. C_4 species are also more successful in warm inland deserts, while C_3 species are more successful in moist, cool coastal habitats.

THE GREENHOUSE EFFECT

In Britain, they call it a glasshouse because they are traditionally covered with glass. But whether they are covered with glass or plastic (as many now are), a greenhouse is a place to grow plants. We can grow plants in a greenhouse because the glass or plastic is transparent to light while helping to retain heat. Earth is also a place to grow plants—instead of glass, there is an atmosphere surrounding Earth that does exactly the same thing.

The atmosphere is composed of a number of gases, including nitrogen, oxygen, argon, and carbon dioxide. These gases all are transparent to light, which allows sunlight to reach the surface biosphere and drive photosynthesis. Certain atmospheric gases, however, are opaque to longer wavelength infrared radiation. Simply put, these gases absorb infrared radiation or heat (Figure 6.6). Principal among the atmospheric gases that absorb heat are water vapor and CO_2. This is why water vapor and carbon dioxide are referred to as "greenhouse gases." Other atmospheric gasses that absorb heat are methane, derived from anaerobic decomposition, and chlorinated fluorocarbons, used in refrigerants and the manufacture of plastic foam.

During daylight hours, approximately 20%–25% of the incoming solar radiation is absorbed by atmospheric water vapor and clouds, roughly half is absorbed by the oceans and landmasses, and the remainder is scattered or reflected back into space. At night, most of the absorbed radiation is re-radiated back toward space as long wavelength infrared radiation or heat that can be absorbed by greenhouse gases in the atmosphere. The atmosphere thus wraps the Earth in a "thermal blanket" that traps heat near the surface of the planet, a phenomenon that prevents extreme overheating of the Earth during the day and excessive cooling at night.

The term *greenhouse effect* was first used by the chemist Svante August Arrhenius in the 19th century, but the phenomenon itself has been around since the beginnings of life on Earth. The greenhouse effect is the principal reason there is liquid water on the Earth's surface and is thus a major factor in determining the fitness of the environment for life. Without the temperature-moderating effects of the atmosphere, water would either be present primarily as ice or vapor—there

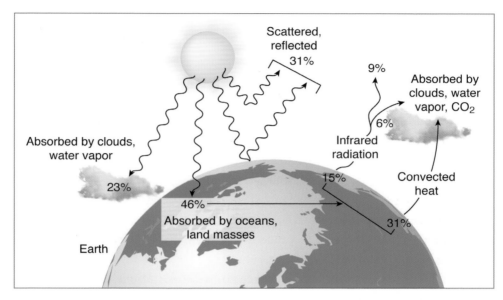

Figure 6.6 Water vapor, CO_2, and other gases in the atmosphere are responsible for the greenhouse effect. About one-quarter of the incoming radiation from the sun is absorbed by atmospheric clouds and water vapor, about one-third is reflected or scattered back into space by clouds and the surface (such as snow), and the rest is absorbed by oceans and landmasses. A portion of the absorbed radiation is recycled back as infrared radiation or convected heat that can be absorbed by water vapor and other greenhouse gases. Higher concentrations of these gases reduce the infrared radiation and heat that can escape into space.

would be little or no liquid water and, consequently, no possibility of life.

The world is currently engaged in a vigorous debate about greenhouse gas emissions and the prospects of global warming. It is a debate charged with emotion that often tends to obscure conflicting evidence. Advocates of the global warming scenario argue that increases in greenhouse gases, CO_2 in particular, will lead to significant increases in global temperatures in the future. Opponents of this view argue that evidence in support of such a scenario is either lacking or contrary and that current warming trends are not caused by human activities but reflect transient changes in the output of the sun or natural, long-term cycles here on Earth. As is often the case, the truth is probably found some-where in the middle.

It is generally agreed that the CO_2 concentration in our atmosphere has been increasing. Up until about 200 years ago, the CO_2 concentration in the atmosphere remained relatively constant at about 0.0275% or 275 parts per million (ppm). Since the beginning of the Industrial Revolution, the atmospheric concentration of CO_2 has increased by roughly 30% to approx-imately 360 ppm (Figure 6.7). Data for the years from the late 1700s up to the 1950s are based on the CO_2 content of ice core samples from the Antarctic. Data from 1958 to the present is based on actual measurements of atmospheric CO_2 over Hawaii and other locations.

Given the timing and progression of this increase in atmo-spheric CO_2, it is assumed that the cause is human activities, such as industrial emissions, burning fossil fuels, and the slash-and-burn practice of clearing forests. What is less certain is if temperatures are actually increasing and, if they are, whether or not the increase in CO_2 is driving those changes. At some climatological stations throughout the United States, the mean annual temperature over the past 70 years has tended to increase, at others it has remained stable, and at yet others it has declined slightly. Even if a correlation between CO_2 levels and temperature can be established, we do not yet know which is cause and which is effect. There are reports that higher temper-atures could accelerate carbon loss from some ecosystems, either by stimulating the microbial breakdown of litter on the forest floor or by thawing deep soil that has held carbon for several thousand years.

The problem with the global warming controversy is that predictions about CO_2 and global warming are based almost exclusively on computer modeling: certain assumptions are made, the assumptions are plugged into a mathematical model, and the program is run to see what the results may be. Computer

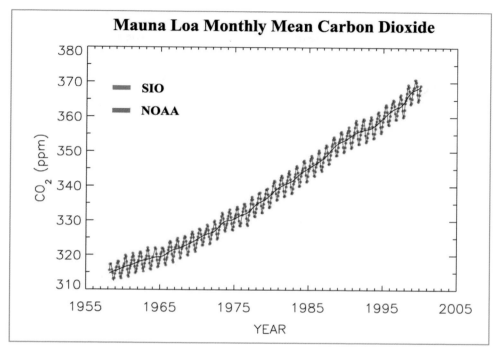

Figure 6.7 The atmospheric concentration of carbon dioxide as measured at the Mauna Loa Observatory in Hawaii. A continuous trend of increasing CO_2 concentration reflects seasonal photosynthetic activity of the terrestrial biosphere in the Northern Hemisphere.

models are only as good as the assumptions built into them and most models are not designed to test whether CO_2 is the culprit, but start with the assumption that CO_2 emissions *are* driving global climate change.

But what about water vapor? The amount of water vapor in the atmosphere is difficult to estimate because it is so highly variable and climate change models do not accommodate this variability well. Let's assume, for the sake of argument, that the water vapor concentration in the atmosphere is 10,000 ppm, a reasonable average. If so, the concentration of total greenhouse gas (water vapor + CO_2) over the past 250 years has increased only 0.73% (from 10,275 ppm to 10,350 ppm). Some computer models again *assume* that higher CO_2 levels will increase water vapor (presumably through increased evaporation driven by higher temperatures), but the validity of this assumption has not been scientifically

Why Is There Snow on the Mountain?

C_4 plant species are not very successful in the cool, moist environment at higher elevations. Have you ever hiked up a mountain and wondered why the air gets cooler and you often encounter fog and clouds the higher you go? After all, you are getting closer to the sun, so why doesn't the air get warmer? And if the air is cooler, why doesn't it descend from the mountain and displace the warmer air in the valley? The answer to these questions has to do with air pressure and a curious phenomenon called adiabatic lapse.

The term *adiabatic* refers to the fact that cooling occurs without an exchange of heat and the term *adiabatic lapse* refers to the change in temperature with increasing elevation. Air temperature is a measure of the average kinetic energy, or heat content, of a unit volume of air. As you travel up a mountainside, the pressure decreases and, consequently, the air mass expands and becomes less dense. There is no loss of heat, but the temperature (heat per unit volume) deceases because the same amount of heat is distributed throughout a larger, expanded volume of air. For dry air, the temperature decreases at about 1°C (1.8°F) for each 100 m (328 feet) in elevation. For moist air, the temperature change is somewhat less because heat is given off when the water vapor condenses to form fog or rain.

In North America, prevailing winds sweep in from the Pacific Ocean and rise up the windward side of the Rocky Mountains. Adiabatic lapse cools the air, water condenses, and rain or snow falls in the mountains. As the dry air descends on the leeward side of the mountains, pressure increases, the volume of air contracts, and the temperature increases—again at the rate of 1°C for each 100 m drop in elevation. This reverse adiabatic lapse is responsible for the warm, dry Chinook winds that blow out of the Rocky Mountains into the eastern foothills.

established. Who is right? Only time and continued efforts to collect hard scientific evidence will provide the answer.

GLOBAL CARBON BUDGET

The conversion of solar energy into organic matter by photosynthesis is the underlying process responsible for all increases in biomass. The total amount of carbon assimilated through photosynthesis worldwide on an annual basis is known as **gross primary productivity** (**GPP**). However, not all of GPP is available for increased biomass because of the amount of carbon that is returned to the atmosphere as a product of respiration. In order to determine the carbon gain that is actually available for an increase in biomass, GPP must be corrected for carbon loss due to respiration. The difference is known as **net primary productivity** (**NPP**). NPP ranges from virtually zero in habitats that are too dry or too cold to support significant plant growth, such as deserts and tundra, to approximately 50 billion metric tons (1 metric ton = 2,205 pounds) in tropical forests (Table 6.1).

Table 6.1 Net Primary Productivity (NPP) and Total Biomass for Selected Ecosystems

Values for NPP are in grams of carbon per square meter per year. Values for total biomass are in million metric tons.

Ecosystem	NPP	Total Biomass
Tropical forests	3,800	1,025
Temperate forests	2,500	385
Northern boreal forests	800	240
Grasslands	1,500	74
Deserts	93	14
Oceans and estuaries	5,000	4

Carbon, principally in the form of CO_2, is in a constant state of flux as it moves between the atmospheric CO_2 pool and various carbon reservoirs (Figure 6.8). This complex exchange of carbon is known as the **Global Carbon Cycle.** Because of increasing interest in the possible links between CO_2 and climate change, efforts are being made to better understand the **global carbon budget**, the size of the major sources and sinks for carbon and the flow of carbon between them. This is not an easy task, given the immense scale and how little we know about the processes that control carbon fluxes. Consequently, the numbers can only be approximations at best.

There are three principal reservoirs of carbon: (1) gaseous CO_2 in the atmosphere, (2) organic carbon in the biosphere, and (3) bicarbonate (HCO_3^-) and carbonate (CO_3^{2-}) in the oceans and sediments. The largest pool of carbon is the oceans, which contain approximately 38,000 billion tons compared with 750 billion tons in the atmospheric pool and slightly less in terrestrial vegetation. The oceanic pool is large because CO_2 reacts with the surface waters to form bicarbonate and carbonate. The CO_2-bicarbonate-carbonate reactions are reversible, however, which means that the oceans and major freshwater lakes tend to buffer the atmospheric CO_2 concentration. When there is excess CO_2 in the atmosphere, more dissolves to form more bicarbonate and carbonate. If there is a local depletion of CO_2 in the atmosphere, bicarbonate releases CO_2 into the atmosphere. The largest CO_2 fluxes are between the atmosphere and terrestrial vegetation and between the atmosphere and the oceans.

The global carbon budget raises one of the more interesting problems facing environmental and atmospheric scientists today. According to the best data available, approximately 6 billion tons of carbon are being added to the atmosphere annually through the combustion of fossil fuels and another 1 billion tons through tropical deforestation. At the same time, the atmospheric pool is increasing by a bit more than 3 billion

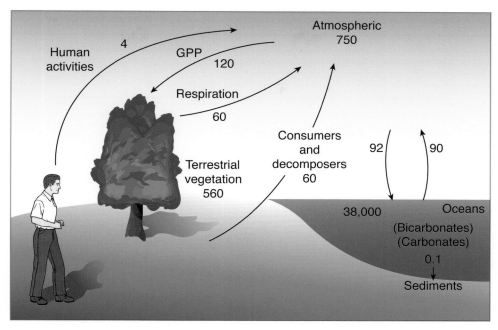

Figure 6.8 The Global Carbon Cycle (above) expresses changes in CO_2 in units of million metric tons. Carbon is in a constant state of flux between the atmospheric pool, terrestrial vegetation, and the oceans. About half of the global primary productivity (GPP) is returned to the atmosphere through plant respiration. Consumers that eat plants and decomposers that break down plant and animal remains carry out respiration that returns carbon to the atmosphere. Oceans buffer the CO_2 content of the atmosphere by absorbing and releasing CO_2.

tons annually and an additional 2 billion tons are sequestered by the oceans. This leaves between 1 and 2 billion tons of unaccounted carbon.

Where is the missing carbon? The most likely possibility seems to be NPP and increased biomass attributed to the re-growth of forests in temperate northern latitudes. An increasing number of studies indicate that forest trees across North America and Europe are capable of responding to CO_2 fertilization just as horticultural crops do in greenhouses. Studies based on satellite imagery have indicated a 6% to 10% increase in global terrestrial NPP over the period from 1987 to 1999, an increase that has been attributed to CO_2 fertilization as well as higher temperatures, higher rainfalls, and aerial nitrogen fertilization from industrial effluents.

Current CO_2 levels are higher than they have been for the past 100,000 years, so it is not possible to extrapolate from past experience, but healthy forests in the biosphere may be able to put the brakes on potential global warming if the CO_2 content of the atmosphere continues to rise.

Summary

A variety of environmental factors are known to influence the rate of photosynthesis and, consequently, plant growth and productivity. The balance between CO_2 uptake by photosynthesis and CO_2 evolution by respiration is referred to as the carbon exchange rate (CER). At the light compensation point, CER is zero; below that, the CER is negative because the rate of photosynthesis is exceeded by the rate of respiration. Photosynthesis continues to increase with more light until it reaches saturation, and then CO_2 becomes the limiting factor. C_4 plants never achieve light saturation, because C_4 plants have minimized photorespiration and continue photosynthesis at very low CO_2 levels. As a result, C_4 plants have a higher water use efficiency and enjoy an advantage over C_3 plants in hot, dry habitats.

An important factor in forest and agricultural ecosystems is canopy structure. An ideal canopy structure optimizes the absorption of light by leaves, while minimizing the number of leaves that receive light near or below the light compensation point. Plants adapt to shade environments with thinner leaves, larger surface areas, and fewer chloroplasts with augmented light harvesting antenna. In bright sun, plants protect against photoinhibition by funneling excess energy to the carotenoid pigments, which dissipate the energy harmlessly as heat.

The greenhouse effect refers to the temperature-moderating effects of water vapor and CO_2 in the atmosphere. By preventing overheating and excess cooling on the Earth's surface, the greenhouse effect ensures that sufficient water is maintained to support life. There is concern that increasing atmospheric CO_2 concentrations may lead to global warming, but there is some evidence that increasing net primary productivity of temperate forest ecosystems may help to moderate the effect.

7 An Evolutionary History of Energy Metabolism

Species do not evolve to perfection, but quite the contrary.
The weak, in fact, always prevail over the strong, not only because
they are in the majority, but also because they are the more crafty.

—Friedrich Nietzsche (1844—1900)
German philosopher, poet

An Evolutionary History of Energy Metabolism

THE FIRST CELLS

As we have seen, the mechanisms of photosynthesis and respiration are fundamentally the same. This is perhaps not surprising, since each is a process for transforming energy and it is likely that any underlying mechanism that does the job would be conserved through evolutionary mechanisms. Both photosynthesis and respiration involve oxidation-reduction reactions and use transmembrane proton pumps to generate ATP, which is the principal energy currency. Apparently all three of these elements—redox reactions, proton pumps, and ATP—arose early in evolutionary history and have been conserved with little change ever since.

We can not be certain what conditions existed on Earth at the time of its formation or through its first few hundred million years. Speculation is that the nascent Earth was a violent place, racked with volcanic eruptions, electrical storms, torrential rains, and strong ultraviolet radiation. It is believed that the atmosphere was rich in hydrogen gas (H_2), ammonia (NH_3), and simple hydrocarbons such as methane (CH_3), but there was no free, or gaseous, oxygen (O_2).

Laboratory experiments designed to simulate these conditions have shown them to be an incubator for the **abiotic** synthesis of numerous organic molecules, such as amino acids, nucleotides, sugars, and simple fatty acids. Fatty acids could have formed the first primitive membranes and amino acids are the building blocks for proteins, while sugars and nucleotides are the building blocks for ATP and nucleic acids. There wasn't a real need for genetic direction in the beginning since simple proteins, polynucleotides, and membranes are all capable of spontaneous self-assembly.

The first living cells are thought to have arisen 3–4 billion years ago. These primitive, bacteria-like cells would have obtained chemical energy by breaking down the hydrogen-rich organic molecules that were abundant in the primeval broth. Given the propensity of amino acids to self-assemble into proteins, it was probably not too long before proteins with catalytic activity began mediating reactions similar to present day fermentation pathways.

In fermentation, reduced organic molecules are only partially oxidized. With no oxygen to serve as the electron acceptor, the electrons removed during oxidation must be transferred to some other molecule, which then becomes reduced. These early electron acceptors may have been similar to NAD^+ or $NADP^+$. Using the free energy of oxidation to synthesize ATP directly, a type of substrate-level phosphorylation was probably also an early development. Overall, the early pathway for substrate oxidation and ATP synthesis probably resembled present-day glycolysis (see Chapter 5).

Most fermentations produce organic acids (carbon compounds that carry a –COOH group) that would have been excreted from the cell as a waste product. Excretion of organic acids would have acidified the cell's immediate environment; that is, it would have increased the proton (H^+) concentration or lowered the pH surrounding the cell. At the same time, the ongoing oxidation reactions in the cell would also release protons and the cell would have had to take steps to prevent acidification of its cytoplasm. Proteins in the cell's membrane would have evolved that used energy to pump protons out of the cell. Since protons were already accumulating in the environment, these additional protons would have to be pumped out against a proton concentration gradient and this would require energy. At least some of those proton pumps could have used ATP as its energy source. An ATP-driven proton pump would have created a significant ATP demand but, as we saw in Chapter 5, fermentation is not very efficient and the ATP yield is small. Fortunately, a more efficient means for producing ATP was waiting in the wings.

PUMPING PROTONS WITH LIGHT

There are not very many organisms that can tolerate the high salt concentration of a typical salt lake, but one that can is *Halobacter halobium. Halobacter* is thought to have originated 3 billion years ago, shortly after the dawn of life. It is a purple bacterium that thrives in salt concentrations more than five times that of sea water. The bacterium inhabits places such as the Dead Sea, where sodium chloride concentrations reach as high as 4.0 molar (sea water is about 0.6 molar sodium chloride). Because few other organisms can survive in this environment, *Halobacter* has remained relatively free of competition and is thought to have retained many of the attributes of primitive cells.

The Origin of Chloroplasts and Mitochondria

Necessity may be the mother of invention, according to an old proverb, but evolution tends to operate more conservatively. If old parts can be modified or rearranged to create something new, then that is the preferred route. This is apparently what happened when the first eukaryotic plants and animals appeared.

The reactions of respiration and photosynthesis in eukaryotic cells are carried out in discrete structures called mitochondria and chloroplasts. Both mitochondria and chloroplasts have DNA and the capacity to synthesize proteins that are distinctly bacterial in character. In addition, there are striking similarities in structure and function between the enzyme complexes that transport electrons and pump protons in the electron transport chains of bacteria, mitochondria, and chloroplasts.

Because of these similarities, it is believed that mitochondria are derived from a respiration-dependent bacterium that resided in a primitive eukaryotic cell. Similarly, chloroplasts arose when a descendent of this early union engulfed a blue-green ancestor of the cyanobacteria.

The pigment that gives *Halobacter* its purple color is called **bacteriorhodopsin**. Bacteriorhodopsin is a **chromoprotein,** which is a protein with an attached group called a chromophore that absorbs light. The cytochromes described earlier are also chromoproteins. The chromophore responsible for the purple color in bacteriorhodopsin is a 20-carbon group called retinal. Bacteriorhodopsin is also an integral transmembrane protein, which means that it spans the membrane with parts of the protein projecting into the aqueous medium on either side.

Halobacter is heterotrophic—it can not grow without a supply of reduced organic substances. However, *Halobacter* does have one advantage over the cells that preceded it—bacteriorhodopsin uses light rather than ATP to pump protons out of the cell. The pigment sits in the cell's outer membrane and when the retinal group absorbs a photon, the absorbed energy causes the protein to change its shape. As its shape changes, the protein pulls a proton from the cytoplasm and releases it outside the cell (Figure 7.1). The result is an energy-rich electrochemical proton gradient across the membrane.

Some of the free energy stored in the gradient is released when protons leak back into the cell. If protons were to leak back into the cell through the ATP-driven proton pumps, the energy could be used to run the pumps in reverse. Reversing the pump would drive the synthesis of ATP rather than its hydrolysis. Bacteriorhodopsin would then set in motion a proton circuit, in which protons pumped out of the cell by the light-driven bacteriorhodopsin pump generated ATP as they returned to the cell. The basic elements of this proton circuit have been conserved in present-day photosynthesis and respiration and form the basis for ATP synthesis.

The energy of the proton gradient established by bacteriorhodopsin could also be linked to the uptake of nutrients from the environment, again as it is in present-day cells. Energy-linked

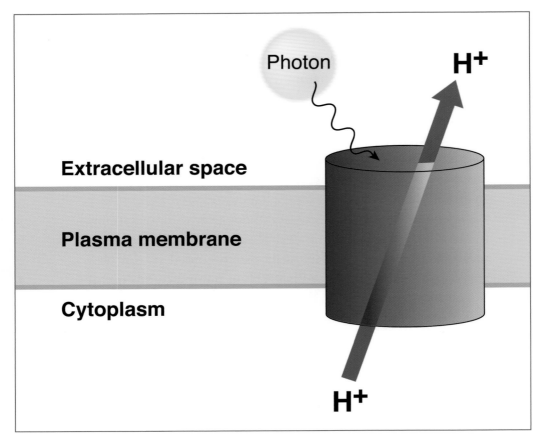

Figure 7.1 Bacteriorhodopsin (bR) forms purple patches in the cell membranes of bacteria such as *Halobacter halobium*. When the chromophore of bacteriorhodopsin absorbs a photon, the absorbed energy induces a change in the shape, or conformation, of the protein. As it changes shape, the protein picks up a proton (H⁺) from the cytoplasm and delivers it to the space outside the cell.

nutrient uptake would become especially important as the concentration of nutrients in the primeval broth declined and nutrients had to taken into the cell from increasingly dilute solutions. Overall, a light-driven proton pump would increase the efficiency of nutrient uptake, provide an almost unlimited supply of ATP for other metabolic needs, and give purple bacteria such as *Halobacter* a decided advantage over earlier life forms.

ANAEROBIC PHOTOSYNTHESIS

The purple bacteria may have been the world's first photosynthetic organism, but they shared with their predecessors one potentially fatal deficiency—they could not fix carbon dioxide. This is a significant limitation for at least two reasons. First, the hydrocarbons in the primeval broth were formed geochemically and the conditions that led to their formation no longer existed, so there was a finite supply. Second, the fermentation reactions that fed on hydrocarbons generated large amounts of carbon dioxide as a waste product. Additional carbon dioxide may also have been contributed to the atmosphere through geochemical processes. With no means for converting this carbon dioxide back into organic carbon, there would inevitably have been a gradual decline in the amount of carbon available to the biosphere. An alternative source of carbon had to be found and the most abundant potential carbon source at the time was the carbon dioxide in the atmosphere.

Carbon dioxide can be converted into organic carbon only by chemical reduction. Reduction of carbon dioxide to sugar requires a particularly strong electron donor such as NADH or its close relative, NADPH. NADH was a product of fermentation, but the dwindling supply of fermentable hydrocarbons meant that NADH supplies were also increasingly limited. It was therefore essential that cells evolve a new way of generating the necessary reducing potential.

The principal breakthrough was the appearance of photochemical reaction centers—organized groups of pigment molecules that could use light energy to produce NADH or NADPH directly. This development is thought to have occurred about 3 billion years ago in ancestors of the present-day green sulfur bacteria. The pigment in the green sulfur bacteria is bacteriochlorophyll, a green pigment similar to the chlorophylls found in green algae and higher plants.

(continued on page 144)

Why Are Leaves Green?

If you were able to construct an ideal photosynthetic pigment, what color would it be? One could argue that the best photosynthetic pigment would absorb light from all portions of the visible spectrum. Such a pigment would allow the plant to utilize all of the light energy available to it. Such a pigment would also be black, so why are leaves green?

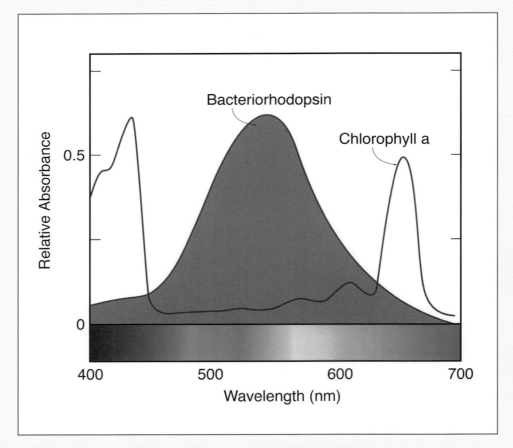

Bacteriorhodopsin absorbs light form the middle of the visible spectrum. When the chlorophylls came on the scene, only light at the blue and red ends of the spectrum—light that is not absorbed by bacteriorhodopsin—was available.

The answer could simply be that *Halobacter halobium* got here first. *Halobacter* is a salt-loving bacterium that uses light collected by the bacteriorhodopsin bacterium. Pigments get their color by selectively absorbing certain portions of the visible spectrum—light that is not absorbed gives pigment its color. The pigment of bacteriorhodopsin, for example, is purple because it absorbs light broadly from the middle of the visible spectrum and allows only light at the red and blue ends of the spectrum to pass through. The eye perceives a mix of red and blue as purple. *Halobacter* was highly successful for awhile and at their peak the Earth might have been covered with purple seas.

When the green anaerobic bacteria first arrived on the scene, they lived on deep water sediments and had to compete with the *Halobacter* swimming above them for available light. It should not be surprising then that the newcomers evolved a pigment that absorbed the leftover red and blue light that *Halobacter* did not use.

Although most of the purple bacteria have long since disappeared and more light from the center of the spectrum is now available, chlorophyll remains the dominant photosynthetic pigment. Most green algae and developed plants are seldom short of light and the chlorophyll-based system serves them well.

Some plants have, however, evolved pigments that recapture some of the light from the middle of the spectrum. One of the best examples is the red algae which tend to grow in deep water where light has difficulty penetrating. In addition to chlorophyll, red algae contain the pigments phycocyanin and phycoerythrin, both of which function as accessory pigments that pass their absorbed light on to chlorophyll for use in photosynthesis. Phycoerythrin, in particular, absorbs strongly in the green region of the spectrum where chlorophyll absorption is minimal. Consequently, red algae may appear almost black because they absorb such a large proportion of the visible radiation.

(continued from page 141)
Bacteriochlorophyll is organized in a photosystem, which is simply a group of pigment and protein molecules that work cooperatively to collect light energy. Each photosystem contains a group of pigment molecules that function as antenna to harvest light energy. This energy is then passed to the reaction center, where the photochemical reduction actually occurs. Photosystems were described in Chapter 4, but for the moment just think of a photosystem as an electron pump that extracts electrons from an electron donor and uses light to raise their energy level.

The first green sulfur bacteria no doubt used a variety of electron donors, but the most successful of them probably used hydrogen sulfide (H_2S) (Figure 7.2). Light absorbed by the bacteriochlorophyll photosystem works with several other molecules to transfer electrons from H_2S (a relatively weak reductant) to $NADP^+$, thereby producing NADPH (a strong reductant). In electrical terms, the effect of light is to increase the voltage of the energized electron.

$$2H_2S + 2NADP^+ + \text{light energy} \longrightarrow 2S + 2NADPH + 2H^+$$

NADPH is then used to reduce carbon dioxide to carbohydrate (CH_2O):

$$CO_2 + 2NADPH + 2H^+ \longrightarrow (CH_2O) + 2S$$

The overall reaction is:

$$CO_2 + 2H_2S + \text{light energy} \longrightarrow (CH_2O) + H_2O + 2S$$

As successful as the green sulfur bacteria might have been, however, they too suffered limitations. Hydrogen sulfide is not universally abundant, so the green sulfur bacteria would have been limited to hot sulfur springs and similar locations.

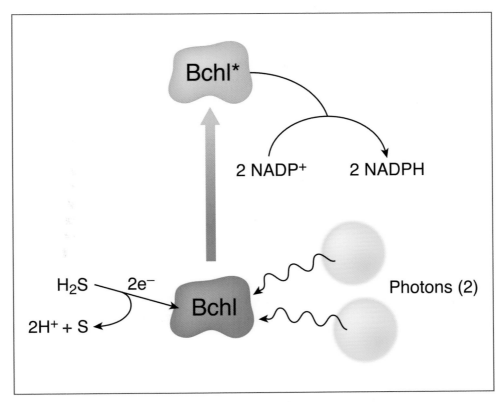

Figure 7.2 The photosystem of the green sulfur bacteria most likely gave rise to the present-day Photosystem I of green plants. (Bchl = bacteriochlorophyll.)

THE FIRST ATMOSPHERIC OXYGEN

The next step in the evolution of photosynthesis was the development of organisms that could use water as an electron source rather than hydrogen sulfide. This step is thought to have originated with the cyanobacteria (blue-green algae) about 2.0–2.5 billion years ago. Using water as a source of electrons was a pivotal step because, unlike hydrogen sulfide, the supply of water was almost unlimited and thus provided an inexhaustible source of reducing power. The new oxygen-evolving organisms could now invade a much broader range of habitats and evolve in ways denied to their predecessors.

Moreover, stripping electrons from water resulted in the production of oxygen, which set the stage for far-reaching advances in aerobic respiration.

This apparently simple step required a sea-change in the photochemical apparatus with significant biological consequences. While a single excitation of chlorophyll was more than enough to overcome the voltage gap between hydrogen sulfide and NADPH (about 90 mV), water has a much lower redox potential and the voltage gap between water and NADPH is correspondingly greater (about 1,140 mV). Bridging this large voltage gap required the addition of a second photosystem acting in series with the first, in much the same way that stacking two batteries in a flashlight doubles the voltage (Figure 7.3).

Based on what is known about the structure of present-day photosystems in bacteria and green plants, it has been suggested that the original electron pump, the one that delivered electrons to $NADP^+$, was derived from the green sulfur bacteria. This photosystem is the one now called photosystem I. The second pump (the present-day photosystem II), which extracted electrons from water and delivered them to photosystem I, was derived from a related organism, the purple sulfur bacteria. Modified versions of earlier electron-carrying enzymes were co-opted to connect the two chains.

With water as the source of electrons and two photosystems operating in series, the overall equation for photosynthesis reached the form that survives today:

$$CO_2 + 2H_2O \longrightarrow (CH_2O) + H_2O + O_2$$

AEROBIC RESPIRATION

In spite of the success of oxygen-evolving photosynthesis, another billion years would pass before atmospheric oxygen levels exceeded a few percent. This slow rise in oxygen level was

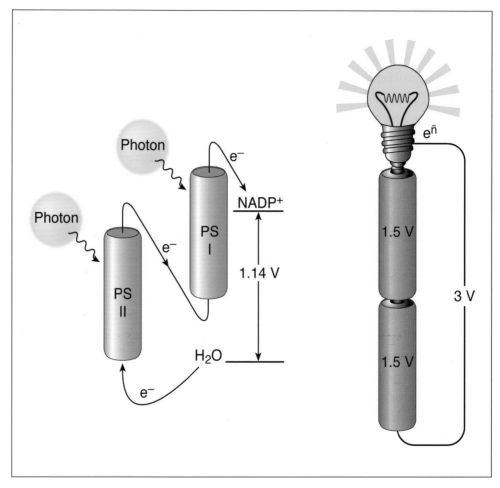

Figure 7.3 Placing two photosystems in a series is like using two 1.5 V batteries to power a 3-V flashlight. Two photons provide the energy required to bridge the voltage gap between water and NADP.

due to large amounts of reduced iron dissolved in the primordial seas. Nearly all the oxygen produced by the early cyanobacteria was precipitated as insoluble ferric oxides. However, after the iron supply was exhausted (about 1.5 billion years ago), atmospheric oxygen levels increased rapidly, reaching current levels about 1 billion years ago.

At about the same time that oxygen levels began to rise and organic material produced through photosynthesis became more widely available, some bacteria found they could forgo photosynthesis and survive entirely by aerobic respiration. By modifying components of existing electron transport chains and proton pumps, and using oxygen as the terminal electron acceptor, these bacteria could make their ATP by breaking down reduced organic materials all the way to carbon dioxide.

The first multicellular plants and animals would not appear for another billion years or so, but the metabolic machinery that they would use for their energy metabolism was already set up and has survived the test of time.

Summary

The evolution of photosynthesis and respiration is marked by a series of major events, each a significant step forward in biological efficiency. The first cells are believed to have been bacteria-like organisms that used a form of fermentation to extract energy from reduced organic molecules. Some of the energy of oxidation was used to form ATP and the need to prevent acidification of the cell's interior led to the evolution of membrane-based proton pumps. Some of these pumps may have been driven by ATP.

The second major event in the evolution of energy metabolism was the advent of a primitive photosynthesis that used light to pump protons out of the cell and used the energy of the proton gradient to synthesize ATP. Protons that leaked back into the cell through an ATP-driven proton pump would cause the synthesis of ATP.

The third major event was the evolution of organized photosystems, or electron pumps, that carried out carbon dioxide reduction using electrons extracted from reduced substrates such as hydrogen sulfide. This provided organisms a partial relief from their dependence on diminishing supplies of reduced compounds that had been formed by geochemical processes. The fourth major event was the substitution of water for hydrogen sulfide as the source of electrons for carbon dioxide reduction. The consequent evolution of oxygen set the stage for aerobic respiration and life as we know it today.

Glossary

Abiotic Inorganic; not involving living organisms.

Absorption spectrum A graph that displays the absorption of light by a pigment as a function of wavelength.

Adenine A nitrogenous base present in nucleotide derivatives such as ADP, ATP, NAD, NADP, and nucleic acids.

Adenosine diphosphate (ADP) A nucleotide consisting of adenine, ribose, and two phosphate groups. Becomes ATP on addition of a third phosphate group.

Adenosine triphosphate (ATP) A nucleotide consisting of adenine, ribose, and three phosphate groups. ATP is the principal energy currency in cells.

Adenylic acid A nucleotide consisting of adenine, ribose, and one phosphate group.

Aerobic Pertaining to the presence of molecular oxygen.

Anaerobic Pertaining to the absence of molecular oxygen.

Antenna pigment A chlorophyll molecule in a photosystem that absorbs photons and passes the excitation energy to the reaction center.

Anthocyanins Water-soluble pigments dissolved in the central vacuole. Usually red, blue, or purple.

ATP synthetase (ATPase) An enzyme in the chloroplast thylakoid membrane or mitochondrial inner membrane that uses the energy of a proton gradient to synthesize ATP from ADP and inorganic phosphate.

Autoradiography A technique for making a photographic print of radioactive substances on a chromatogram.

Bacteriorhodopsin A purple chromoprotein found in the cell membranes of bacteria such as *Halobacter halobium*, where it serves as a light-driven proton pump.

Beta-carotene The principal carotenoid in chloroplasts.

Bioenergetics The study of thermodynamic principles to help explain the flow of energy through living organisms.

Biosphere The air, land, and water at the surface of the Earth where organisms live.

Bundle sheath A ring of cells that tightly surrounds a vascular bundle (or vein) in a leaf. Bundle sheaths are particularly well-developed in leaves of C_4 plants.

C_3 plants Plants that fix carbon exclusively by the photosynthetic carbon reduction cycle.

C_4 plants Plants that fix carbon using a combination of the phospho-enolpyruvate pathway and the C_3 pathway.

Calvin cycle Another name for the photosynthetic carbon reduction cycle.

Carbon exchange rate (CER) The balance between CO_2 uptake for photosynthesis and CO_2 evolution from photorespiration and cellular respiration.

Carotenes Orange pigments found in chloroplasts or chromoplasts and members of the carotenoid family of pigments. Carotenes are fat-soluble hydrocarbons composed entirely of carbon and hydrogen.

Carotenoids A family of fat-soluble pigments that includes the carotenes and xanthophylls.

Cellular respiration A process in which molecules are oxidized with a release of energy.

Chemiosmotic coupling A mechanism for coupling ATP synthesis to electron transport through an electrochemical proton gradient across a chloroplast or mitochondrial membrane.

Chlorophyll The primary photosynthetic pigment in plants, algae, and bacteria. From the Greek *Chloros,* meaning "green," and *phyllon,* meaning "leaf."

Chloroplasts Microscopic structures in the cells of leaves that contain the pigment chlorophyll, which absorbs incoming solar energy.

Chromatogram A sheet of paper on which molecules have been separated by the technique of paper chromatography.

Chromoprotein A protein with an attached group that absorbs light and gives the protein color. The light-absorbing group is called a chromatophore. Bacteriorhodopsin, cytochromes, and hemoglobin are examples of chromoproteins.

Glossary

Citric acid cycle (CAC) The second of three pathways in cellular respiration, in which pyruvate is oxidized to carbon dioxide. Also known as the Krebs cycle or the tricarboxylic acid cycle (TCA cycle).

Coenzyme A non-protein organic molecule that plays an essential accessory role in an enzyme reaction. NAD and FAD are examples of coenzymes.

Crassulacean acid metabolism (CAM) A variation of the C_4 cycle in which PEP carboxylase fixes carbon at night and stores it as organic acids in the central vacuole of the cell. During the day, the carbon is refixed by the PCR cycle in the same cell.

Crista (plural, cristae) An infolding of the mitochondrial inner membrane, containing the components of the electron transport chain and oxidative phosphorylation.

Cuticle A waxy deposit on the outer leaf surfaces of plants. It is impervious to water, so it prevents evaporation of water from the surfaces of the epidermal cells and thus protects the plant from potentially lethal desiccation.

Cyclic electron transport Light-driven electron flow in which the electrons originate in photosystem I and return to photosystem I through the cytochrome complex.

Cyclic photophosphorylation ATP formation associated with cyclic electron transport.

Cytochrome An iron-containing heme protein serving as an electron carrier in photosynthesis and cellular respiration.

Cytochrome complex A principal electron transport intermediate in photosynthesis and respiration.

Dark reactions The second stage of photosynthesis; a set of slower, light-independent, enzyme-catalyzed reactions, which use the chemical energy produced during the first-stage light reactions to convert carbon dioxide to sugar.

Dihydroxyacetone phosphate (DHAP) A triose sugar. One of the products of carbon fixation in the PCR cycle.

Electron transport chain The final set of pathways in cellular respiration, in which electrons extracted from glycolysis and the citric acid cycle are passed down a series of redox carriers to oxygen. The principal ATP generator in the cell.

Endergonic reaction A chemical reaction that requires an input of energy to proceed.

Entropy Energy in a form that is not available to do any further work.

Epidermis A layer of cells that covers the two surfaces of a leaf. These cells are very tightly packed with no intercellular spaces and their principal function is to provide mechanical protection.

Excited pigment A pigment that has absorbed a photon.

Exergonic reaction A chemical reaction that proceeds spontaneously. Exergonic reactions release free energy as they proceed.

Fatty acid A long chain (12–20 carbons) hydrocarbon with a terminal carboxyl (acid) group. A principal constituent of fats and oils.

Fermentation The anaerobic breakdown of glucose.

Ferredoxin A small iron-protein that serves as the primary electron acceptor in photosystem I.

Fluorescence The phenomenon whereby light is emitted when an excited pigment returns to the ground state.

Free energy Energy that is available to do work.

Global carbon budget The size of the major sources and sinks for carbon in the biosphere and the flow of carbon between them. There are three principal reservoirs of carbon: (1) gaseous CO_2 in the atmosphere, (2) organic carbon in the biosphere, and (3) bicarbonate and carbonate in the oceans and sediments.

Global Carbon Cycle The exchange of carbon between the atmospheric CO_2 pool and various carbon reservoirs.

Glyceraldehyde-3-phosphate (G3P) The reduced form of 3-phospho-glyceric acid. The product of the reduction stage in the PCR cycle.

Glycolysis The first of three pathways that make up cellular respiration. The steps leading from glucose to pyruvic acid.

Gross primary productivity (GPP) The total amount of carbon assimilated through photosynthesis worldwide on an annual basis.

Ground state The stable condition of a pigment that has not been excited by a photon.

Glossary

Isotope One of several forms of a chemical element that differ only by the number of neutrons in the nucleus but have the same chemical properties.

Kranz anatomy The wreath-like arrangement of cells that surrounds the vascular bundle in the leaf of a C_4 plant.

Leaf area index (LAI) The ratio of the leaf area (one surface only) of a crop to the ground area.

Light A form of energy that can behave either as a wave or as a particle.

Light compensation point When the carbon exchange rate reaches zero.

Light-harvesting complex An additional antenna system that helps to collect photons in dim light or shade.

Light reactions The first stage of photosynthesis; a set of rapid, light-dependent reactions that convert light energy to chemical energy.

Lumen The space inside the thylakoid.

Lycopene A red pigment of the carotenoid family; found in tomatoes.

Matrix The unstructured interior of a mitochondrion, containing the enzymes of the citric acid cycle.

Mitochondrion The cellular organelle in which the aerobic portion of cellular respiration occurs.

Mole The amount of a substance, in grams, equal to its molecular weight.

Net primary productivity (NPP) The total amount of carbon assimilated through photosynthesis worldwide on an annual basis corrected for carbon loss due to respiration.

Nicotinamide adenine dinucleotide (NAD) A common electron carrier involved in photosynthesis.

Nicotinamide adenine dinucleotide phosphate (NADP) A common electron carrier involved in photosynthesis.

Non-cyclic electron transport Electron transport from water to NADH, involving both photosystem II and photosystem I and the cytochrome complex.

Non-cyclic photophosphorylation Light-driven synthesis of ATP associated with non-cyclic electron transport.

Nucleotide A molecule consisting of a nitrogenous base, ribose or deoxyribose sugar, and phosphate.

Obligate anaerobe An organism that is unable to survive in the absence of molecular oxygen.

Oxidation A loss of one or more electrons.

Oxidation-reduction (redox) A chemical reaction involving the exchange of electrons between molecules.

Oxidative phosphorylation The formation of ATP from ADP and inorganic phosphate associated with the passage of electrons to molecular oxygen in the electron transport chain.

Palisade mesophylls Internal leaf cells located on the upper side that contain a large number of chloroplasts and are responsible for most of the photosynthesis that occurs in the leaf.

Paper chromatography A technique for resolving mixtures of molecules.

Pheophytin (Pheo) A chlorophyll molecule lacking a magnesium ion. The primary electron acceptor for photosystem II.

Phosphoenolpyruvate carboxylase (PEPcase) The enzyme that catalyzes the incorporation of carbon dioxide into organic carbon in the mesophyll cells during the C_4 photosynthetic cycle.

Phosphorylation The addition of a phosphate group (PO_4^{3-}) to any molecule.

Photoinhibition A decline in photosynthetic efficiency due to the damaging effects of excess light.

Photon (from the Greek *photos* meaning "light") A quantum of visible radiation.

Photooxidation A light-driven loss of an electron by a molecule such as chlorophyll.

Photoperiodism The response of an organism to seasonal changes.

Photorespiration A process that leads to the light-dependent evolution of carbon dioxide.

Glossary

Photosynthetic carbon reduction cycle The pathway for fixing carbon dioxide as phosphoglyceric acid. Also known as the Calvin cycle or Calvin-Benson cycle.

Photosystem A collection of chlorophyll, carotenoid, and protein molecules that cooperate in collecting and processing photons. Green plants have two photosystems, PSI and PSII. Also known as photosynthetic units.

Phototropism Bending toward or away from the light.

Pigment Any molecule that absorbs light.

Protochlorophyll A chlorophyll-like molecule that is converted to chlorophyll when exposed to light.

Proton motive force (**pmf**) The force generated by a combination of proton gradient and potential difference across a membrane. Work must be done to pump protons against the proton motive force, and work can be done by the force when it collapses.

Proton pump A transmembrane protein that moves protons across a membrane against a concentration gradient or proton motive force.

Pyruvate dehydrogenase The enzyme complex that converts pyruvate into acetyl coenzyme A in preparation to enter the citric acid cycle.

Quantum (plural, quanta) A particle of electromagnetic radiation.

Reaction center The chlorophyll molecule and associated proteins in a photosystem where the actual conversion of light energy to chemical energy takes place.

Reduction The gain of an electron.

Refraction The bending of light waves as they pass from one medium into another.

Ribose A five-carbon sugar.

Rubisco An acronym for the enzyme ribulose-1,5-bisphosphate carboxylase. Also known as ribulose-1,5-bisphosphate carboxylase-oxygenase.

Senescence The process of ageing and, ultimately, dying.

Spongy mesophylls Cells located inside the leaf and below the palisade mesophylls that are irregular in shape and surrounded by a system of interconnected air spaces. The air spaces facilitate gas exchange, such as the uptake of carbon dioxide and the release of oxygen.

Starch Glucose molecules linked end-to-end. It is formed in the chloroplast stroma, where it accumulates as insoluble aggregates.

Stomata (singular, stoma) Microscopic pores found in both the upper and lower epidermis of leaves. Their function is to circumvent the diffusion barrier imposed by the cuticle and allow atmospheric carbon dioxide to diffuse into the internal air spaces of the leaf.

Stroma The homogeneous region inside the leaf in which the thylakoids are embedded. The principal constituents are proteins, most of which are enzymes of the carbon fixation cycle.

Substrate-level phosphorylation The formation of ATP from ADP and inorganic phosphate without the involvement of a proton gradient, or the formation of ATP from ADP by the direct transfer of a phosphate group from a phosphorylated intermediate.

Succulent plants A plant with fleshy, water-storing stems and leaves (e.g., a cactus).

Sucrose A 12-carbon sugar that is a major product of photosynthesis in green leaves; it is also the principal form of sugar that is transported over long distances from leaves to stems and roots in most plants. Also known as common table sugar.

Thermodynamics The physical science that describes the flow of energy and its various transformations. The term reflects the early interest in studying heat, although the principles are broadly applicable to all forms of energy.

3-Phosphoglyceric acid (PGA) A three-carbon organic acid. The first stable product of photosynthesis.

Thylakoids Internal membranes of chloroplasts, these flattened sacs traverse the chloroplast from one end to the other and contain the chlorophyll. They are the site of the light reactions of photosynthesis.

Transmembrane protein A membrane protein that extends across the membrane with access to the aqueous medium on both sides.

Glossary

Transpiration The diffusion of water vapor out of a leaf.

Triose phosphate A three-carbon sugar carrying a phosphate group.

Turgor The condition of a cell being firm or swollen due to water uptake. The opposite of flaccid.

Wavelength The distance between peaks in a continuous wave.

Xanthophylls Yellow pigments of the carotenoid family. Xanthophylls differ from carotenes by having oxygen as a part of their molecular structure.

Xerophytic habitat An arid or water-deficient habitat (e.g., a desert).

Books and Articles

Alberts, B., et al. *Molecular Biology of the Cell*. New York: Garland Publishing, 2002.

Bazzaz, F. A., and E. D. Fajer. "Plant Life in a Carbon Dioxide Rich World." *Scientific American* 266(1992): 68–74.

Campbell, N. A., and J. B. Reece. *Biology*. Sixth edition. Philadelphia: Benjamin Cummings, 2001.

Galston, A. W. *Life Processes of Plants*. New York: Scientific American Library, 1994.

Gold, T. *The Deep Hot Biosphere*. New York: Springer-Verlag, 1999.

Goldsworthy, A. "Why Trees are Green." *New Scientist* (December 1987).

Govindjee, and W. J. Coleman. "How Plants Make Oxygen." *Scientific American* 262(1990): 50–58.

Hall, D. O., and K. K. Rao. *Photosynthesis*. New York: Cambridge University Press, 1999.

Heppner, F. H. *Professor Farnsworth's Explanations in Biology*. New York: McGraw-Hill, 1990.

Hopkins, W. G., and N. P. A. Hüner. *Introduction to Plant Physiology*. Third edition New York: John Wiley & Sons, 2004.

Raven, P. H., R. F. Evert, and S. E. Eichhorn. *Biology of Plants*. New York: Worth Publishers, 1999.

Wilkins, M. *Plant Watching*. New York: Facts on File, 1988.

Websites

Botany

Botany Online—The Internet Hypertextbook
http://www.biologies.uni-hamburg.de/b-online/e00/contents.htm

Kimball's Biology Pages
http://users.rcn.com/jkimball.ma.ultranet/BiologyPages

Photosynthesis

"Introduction to Photosynthesis"
www.mit.edu:8001/afs/athena/course/other/esgbio/www/ps/intro.html

"The Photosynthetic Process"
http://www.life.uiuc.edu/govindjee/paper/gov.html

"Photosynthesis"
http://www.emc.maricopa.edu/faculty/farabee/BIOBK/BioBookPS.html

ASU Center for the Study of Early Events in Photosynthesis.
http://photoscience.la.asu.edu/photosyn/study.html

Cellular Respiration

Oracle® ThinkQuest Library
http://library.thinkquest.org/C004535/cellular_respiration.html

Images of Plant Cells and Organelles

University of Wisconsin—Madison, Department of Botany
http://botit.botany.wisc.edu/images/

Carbon Cycle, Greenhouse Effect, and Global Warming

CO_2 Science
http://www.co2science.org

Earth Observatory
http://earthobservatory.nasa.gov/Library/CarbonCycle/carbon_cycle3.html

Associations

Botanical Society of America
http:/www.

American Society of Plant Biologists
http://www.aspb.org

Journals

American Journal of Botany
http://www.amjbot.org

Plant Physiology
http://www.plantphysiol.org

Index

Index

Index

Reaction centers, 53–58, 62, 119, 144
Refraction, 44
Relative humidity (RH), 21
Respiration
    aerobic, 146–49
    cellular, 90–109, 112–13
    defined, 7–8, 29–30
    function, 7–8, 22, 90, 107, 136, 138–39
    mechanisms, 115, 136
    types, 6–8, 41, 129, 131–32, 148
RH. *See* Relative humidity
Ribose, 37
Rotenone, 106
Rubisco
    reaction, 70–73, 75–76, 78, 82, 86, 123

Senescence, 115
Shade, 117–20
Solar energy. *See* Light energy
Spectrophotometer, 48
Starch, 84–87, 90, 108
Substrate-level phosphorylation, 58,
    101, 137
Succulent plants, 83
Sucrose, 84–87
Sugar
    functions, 7
    production, 10–11, 23, 30–31, 34,
      38–40, 62, 81, 84–85, 109
    reactions, 66–69, 73–74, 90, 141

Sun
    energy of, 26–27, 32–33, 40–41, 55,
      115, 124–25
    harvesting of, 4–23, 117–19

Thermodynamics
    laws of, 27–32, 40–41
Thermonuclear reactions, 26
Thylakoid membranes
    function, 15–17, 52–53, 59–61, 94,
      105–6
    lumen, 15, 59–63, 93–94
Transmembrane protein, 59
Transpiration
    and photosynthesis, 19–23, 82
    and water loss, 18–23
Tricarboxylic acid cycle. *See* Citric acid
    cycle
Triose phosphates, 84

Ubiquinone (UQ), 105–6
UQ. *See* Ubiquinone

Watson, James, 4
Wavelength
    absorption, 44–48, 50, 53, 124

Xanthophylls, 51
Xerophytic habitats, 83

page:

13: © Peter Lamb
15: © Dr. Robert Calentine/
Visuals Unlimited
16: © Dr. Wolf H. Fahrenbach/
Visuals Unlimited
16: © Peter Lamb
20: © Dr. Richard Kessel &
Dr. Gene Shih/Visuals Unlimited
35: © Peter Lamb
36: © Peter Lamb
38: © Peter Lamb
45: © Peter Lamb
49: © Peter Lamb
50: © Peter Lamb
54: © Peter Lamb
57: © Peter Lamb
60: © Peter Lamb
67: © Peter Lamb
69: © Peter Lamb
77: © Peter Lamb

79: © Dr. Ken Wagner/
Visuals Unlimited
80: © Peter Lamb
92: © Peter Lamb
93: © Dr. Martha J. Powell/
Visuals Unlimited
95: © Peter Lamb
99: © Peter Lamb
106: © Peter Lamb
119: © Peter Lamb
121: © Peter Lamb
125: © Peter Lamb
127: Courtesy the National Oceanic
and Atmospheric Administration
(NOAA)
131: © Peter Lamb
140: © Peter Lamb
142: © Peter Lamb
145: © Peter Lamb
147: © Peter Lamb

About the Author

William G. Hopkins received a B.A. in biology from Wesleyan University and a Ph.D. in botany from Indiana University. His post-doctoral training was conducted at Brookhaven National Laboratories. He has taught at Bryn Mawr College and the University of Western Ontario, where he is now professor emeritus of biology. Dr. Hopkins has taught primarily in the areas of plant physiology and cell biology, was responsible for design and implementation of an honors program in cell biology, and served many years as an undergraduate counselor. In 1988, Dr. Hopkins was awarded the university's Gold Medal for Excellence in Teaching. He has served in numerous administrative posts, including several years as chair of the university's Academic Review Board. His research and publications have focused on the role of light and temperature in plant development, the organization of chlorophyll-protein complexes, and energy transformations in chloroplasts. Dr. Hopkins has been a contributing author to two high school biology textbooks and is the senior author of *Introduction to Plant Physiology*.